WORKING
WITH NEPA

Environmental Impact Analysis
for the Resource Manager

By
Peter E. Black
Lee P. Herrington

SUNY at Syracuse
College of Environmental
Science and Forestry

MSS Information Corporation
655 Madison Avenue, New York, N.Y. 10021

Library of Congress Cataloging in Publication Data

Black, Peter E
  Working with NEPA.

  Bibliography.
  Includes index.
  1. Environmental law — United States. 2. Environmental impact statements. I. Herrington, Lee Pierce, joint author. II. Title.
KF3775.B46   353.008'232   74-23639
ISBN 0-8422-0483-0

DEDICATION

to the memory of the man
who wrote the first definitive
environmental impact statement,
George Perkins Marsh

PREFACE

The purpose of this book is to provide a broad-based study of the institutional context, the practical implications of, and the opportunities and challenges presented by Section 102(2)C of the National Environmental Policy Act of 1969.

The material from which this book has been compiled from a variety of sources and from the notes of a number of individuals who assisted us in the presentation of an original course in Environmental Impact to a group of Senior students in the Resources Management Curriculum at the State University of New York College of Environmental Science and Forestry. It is intended that this volume will be used for this course, and for short courses for professional field and office personnel in resources management, and for citizens wherever there is an interest in environmental impact statements. The material presumes a substantial background in ecology on the part of the student, but we have included at the appropriate location in the text references and suggestions for further study of ecological concepts, as well as a summary of principles we feel basic to understanding environmental impact. A companion volume of selected readings is available from the same publisher, and is entitled *Selected Readings in Environmental Impact*.

To complete our project, it is obviously advisable to present an example of an environmental impact statement: One of our own making is indeed in the Appendix. We realize that there can be no single, set format, but suggest that the format we use in presenting Chapters III and IV itself is a useful one, primarily because it permits readers with varying degrees of time and technical expertise to delve into the complex problems of environmental impact to the limits of understanding and to whatever extent desired.

Finally, as is evident from the tone of our presentation, we firmly believe that, although the initial post-NEPA years have been characterized by the use of Section 102(2)C in an obstructionist fashion, our survival depends upon responsible and constructive use of this most important piece of legislation.

P. E. Black
L. P. Herrington

Syracuse, New York
September, 1974

CONTENTS

INTRODUCTION

On January 1, 1970, the National Environmental Policy Act (NEPA), PL91-190, became part of the law of the land. This Act consisted of both a statement of national environmental policy and a provision for an effecting mechanism. Title I of the Act declares the policy in spirit and, in violation of the traditional concept of what constitutes a "good law," imposes new requirements on already existing units of government, namely the preparation of impact statements. Title II of the Act provides for the establishment of a Council on Environmental Quality to advise the President on matters pertaining to the environment, to recommend legislation, and to generally oversee the workings of all that NEPA seeks to implement. This law has triggered a great deal of concern because of the requirement for environmental impact statements; that is, statements which delineate the impact any Federal or federally authorized or funded action will have on the environment.

The simple wording of NEPA has left the door open to serious questioning of the intent of Congress. As a result, there have been and will be extensive course conflicts in an attempt to delineate the requirements of the law.

Simultaneously with the activity in the legal world there has been considerable attention devoted in the scientific world in an attempt to find both a cohesive way of modeling the environment and to provide the data which such models require.

Preparation of the impact statement itself poses problems. The Impact statement for the Alaskan Pipeline consists of 9 volumes, 6 of which deal with environmental concerns. This voluminous amount of written material would be virtually impossible to comprehend. It is evident that some efficient, concise and understandable form of expressing the environmental impact is needed.

We feel that the environmental impact statements as required by Section 102 of the Act can be beneficially and constructively utilized at all levels of government responsible for resources management. The environmental impact statement forces agencies or individuals tampering with various ecosystems to step back and take a look at what they may be doing to the complex webs of the ecosystem.

It is the purpose of this text to delve into four aspects of the environmental impact statement situation; the history, content, and legal interpretation of NEPA and its impact statement policy, the manner in which the impact statement is written, the ecological basis of the statements, and finally the use of the impact statement.

THE HISTORY, CONTENT, AND LEGAL INTERPRETATION OF NEPA AND ITS IMPACT STATEMENT POLICY

There is no doubt that the National Environmental Policy Act is a logical development in the history of resources management in the United States. Not only have environmental concerns been expressed by a number of individuals and organizations, but there have been several acts involving more than lip service to environmental concern in both State and National legislation. Both the legal and historical development of watershed management and air pollution control are central to this history.

Tenor of the Times

Environmental concerns have been expressed by a number of individuals and these concerns have had several impacts on resources development. Some selected quotes illustrate a historical perspective on changing attitudes:

One hundred years ago, George Perkins Marsh (1802-1882) published the book which, in its title, asserted what it has taken us ever since to be convinced of: *The Earth as Modified by Human Action* (Marsh, 1874) was a detailed environmental impact statement---the first one. But it suffered from excessive detail and a style that was difficult to understand. It was ahead of its time. It is worth taking a brief look at some of this remarkable man's observations:

> But it is certain that man has reacted upon organized and inorganic nature, and thereby modified ... the material structure of his earthly home. ... We cannot always distinguish between the results of man's action and the effects of purely geological or cosmical causes. ...But man is everywhere a disturbing agent.

> Wherever he plants his foot, the harmonies of nature
> are turned to discords. ... Man ... extends his
> action over vast spaces, his revolutions are swift
> and radical, and his devastations are, for an almost
> incalculable time after he has withdrawn the arm
> that gave the blow, irreparable. ... But our in-
> ability to assign definite values to these causes
> of the disturbance of natural arrangements is not
> a reason for ignoring the existence of such causes
> in any general view of the relations between man
> and nature, and we are never justified in assuming
> a force to be insignificant because its measure is
> unknown, or even because no physical effect may be
> traced to its origin.

Whereas Marsh overstated his case, John Wesley Powell (1834-
1902), a uniquely sensitive individual, was more pragmatic and
actually brought many of his ideas to bear on the development of
the West. He was a tireless, courageous explorer whose intense
desire to assist mankind in charting both the geography and a
progressive future for the Colorado River was countered with
sensitivity for the exquisiteness of his surroundings:

> This delicate foliage covers the rocks all about
> the fountain, and gives the chamber great beauty.
> But we have little time to spend on admiration, so
> on we go,

he wrote, and sailed on, indeed, to lay the foundations for the
Geological Survey and the Bureau of Reclamation which agency has
since relegated some of the beautiful areas Powell described
to the bottom of a reservoir (Porter, 1969).

John Muir (1838-1914), in contrast, was the preservationist
representing many who foresaw the end result of uncontrolled
and ruthless exploitation: he inspired and was inspired by the
great parklands of the West. His intense love for the land is
aptly expressed in his own words:

> I will follow my instincts; be myself for good or
> ill and see what will be the upshot. As long as
> I live, I'll hear waterfalls and birds and winds
> sing. I'll interpret the rocks, learn the language
> of flood, storm, and avalanche. I'll acquaint
> myself with the glaciers and wild gardens and get
> as near the heart of the world as I can (Swift, 1962).

These individuals and others inspired the resources management professions. Leader among the new professionals was Gifford Pinchot (1865-1946), the first United States forester in training, spirit, and action. He was often at odds with Muir, in that he saw the natural resources as the cornerstone of our existence, though not without some concern for environmental quality:

> The first duty of the human race on the material side
> is to control the use of the earth and all that
> therein is. Conservation means the wise use of the
> earth and its resources for the lasting good of men.
> Conservation is the foresighted utilization, preser-
> vation, and/or renewal of forests, waters, lands,
> and minerals, for the greatest good of the greatest
> number for the longest time (Pinchot, 1947).

Maturing in the generation of this growing professionalism, Robert Marshall (1901-1939) was appalled at the devastation of the forests which he saw. He appealed to the people to nation-alize the forests, for he saw no other way to prevent environmental destruction. Realizing that such a drastic action would take some time, he pleaded for regulation of practices on forest private land because:

> public opinion is so conservative that before
> socializing can be carried out, most of the forest
> lands will be devastated or at least their pro-
> ductivity will be seriously depleted (Marshall, 1930).

His pleadings were not dismissed lightly, for it is certain that the threat of governmental control accelerated the day when American forest industries sought to improve their practices through the Keep Green movement, tree farms, and more locally-(State)-applied forest practice acts.

Mid-Century writers (Vogt, 1948; Osborn, 1948; Gustafson, *et al*, 1949; Brown, 1954; Lyons, 1955; Gyle, 1957; Dasmann, 1962) expanded on and succeeded in illustrating the Malthusian Doctrine in a society of exploding birth rates, growing technology, and developing countries around the world. Stewart L. Udall (1920-   ) translated and implemented many of these ideas into governmental action. He invoked his great predecessors in putting a new perspective on the dilemma of exploitation versus preservation, the heart and soul of NEPA:

> As George Perkins Marsh pointed out a century ago, greed and shortsightedness are conservation's mortal enemies ... but most of our major problems will not be resolved unless the resource interrelationships are evaluated with an eye on long-term gains and long-term values. ...If we are to preserve both the beauty and the bounty of the American earth, it will take thoughtful planning and day-in and day-out effort by business, by government, and by the voluntary organizations. ...the conservation movement can become a sustained, systematic effort both to produce and to preserve. ...Once we decide that our surroundings need not always be subordinated to payrolls and profits based on short-term considerations, there is hope that we can both reap the bounty of the land and preserve an inspiriting environment. ...Those who decide must consider immediate needs, compute the values of competing proposals, and keep distance in their eyes as well (Udall, 1963).

Spurred on by these and a host of other dedicated individuals and by growing concern on the part of the public, the students in colleges and universities provided the prime moving force behind the staging of the first Earth Day on April 22, 1970. This event, in turn, rode the crest of a wave of environmental concern into the Decade of the Seventies, initiated by the President's action of signing NEPA on January 1, 1970.

Legislative History

Parallel to and influenced by the philosophies of these leaders of contemporary thought, was the development of a body of legislation reflecting the gradual shift from uncontrolled exploitation to responsible management of natural resources (USDA, 1952).

Although short-lived in terms of actual practice, William Penn's 1681 ordinance requiring that for every 5 acres of land cleared, 1 acre be left in forest is the first expression of preservation of the natural environment in the Country.

New York State was the first to practice public forest administration, creating a forest reserve in 1885. Many other states followed with varying degrees of restriction on forest practices aimed at preserving environmental quality while permitting forest utilization.

Specific federal lands were set aside in 1872 and 1891 as parks and forests, respectively, for administration later under agencies which did not then exist. The National Park Service and Forest Service later became the administrators of these lands.

In 1905 the forest reserves were transferred from the Department of the Interior to the Department of Agriculture (33 Stat 626)[1]/ and the Forest Service was created (33 Stat 872). This and later legislative developments formalized philosophies and practices which have characterized the Forest Service since that time, thus exemplifying the influence of Pinchot and his contemporaries on modern resources management.

The Weeks Act (16 USC 480, 1911) provided the infant Forest Service with the opportunity to expand the National Forest system. This was justified on the basis of the commerce clause of the Constitution which reserved the right of control over interstate commerce (navigation) to the Federal government. Throughout the eastern states where forest cutting was followed by disasterous floods, forests were alleged to influence runoff, hence the necessity to control the headwaters of navigable streams.

The Antiquities Act (39 Stat 535, 1916) creating the Park Service, admonished that agency to preserve for the use and enjoyment of future generations those areas under its jurisdiction, thus assuring their preservation in some semblance of natural balance. This contradictory admonition confronted the Park Service with a colossal dilemma which persists today. This very contradiction appears also in the current principles and standards for

---

1/ legal referencing style is, for cases, precise name of *plaintiff v. defendant,* underlined or italicized; followed by volume number of court-reporting series (abbreviations standardized, such as S.C. for Supreme Court, F.2d, for Federal Second, etc.); followed by page number in that volume; followed by additional citations for particularly important cases, and finally, the date of the decision. For statutes, the name of the statute is followed by the Public Law number, or the volume number, volume abbreviation, page number, and date.

the evaluation of water and related land resources projects as compiled by the Water Resources Council (1973) and is, of course, the basic problem that NEPA tries to resolve.

But, legislative activities were not restricted to the land resources: The Federal Power Act (16 USC 791, 1920) specified that the Federal Power Commission could grant licenses for power dams only if those dams were part of a comprehensive plan which considered purposes other than power, including recreation.

The Fish and Wildlife Coordination Act (60 Stat 855) of 1946 required that a project-sponsoring agency submit its plans to the Fish and Wildlife Service, but no feedback to the sponsoring agency was provided for. The amendment in 1958 (72 Stat 563) provided for the inclusion of recommendations for the Fish and Wildlife Service with regard to the impact of dams and other river basin projects upon fauna. In the words of the Council of Environmental Quality (1971) the Act "bars water resource projects undertaken by a Federal agency, or with a Federal permit, from running roughshod over wildlife."

Ensuring balanced resource management on the land, the Multiple Use and Sustained Yield Act of 1960 (16 USC 528) largely rubber-stamped existing practice. It required the Forest Service to combine environmental and economic purposes in National Forest Administration. This new requirement has a parallel thread with river basin projects as described below. A similar piece of legislation, the Multiple Use Act of 1964 (PL 86-607) accomplished the same for the Bureau of Land Management.

The 1966 Department of Transportation Act (49 USC 1651) applied these same principles to the bourgeoning problems associated with road-building. It charged the Federal Highway Administration to direct special emphasis toward "preserving along highways the natural beauty of the countryside, public parks, and recreation lands, wildlife and waterfowl refugees, and historic sites"(Office of the Federal Register, 1971).

Attempts to evaluate environmental factors can draw on the several decades of information available in the area of river basin programs and water resources projects as well as on the foregoing laws. White (1972) points out that "It should be recalled that the Section 102 (NEPA) type of statement builds upon the experience of 35 years with Federal review of water management projects." The milestones in this history are as follows:

The 1936 Omnibus Flood Control Act (33 USC 701) laid the foundations of the benefit-cost analysis by stating that a project was to be considered feasible when "the benefits, to whomsoever they may accrue, are in excess of the estimated costs." Although it was not possible under such a vague charge to assess the worth of human life or national defense, such were to be included. The monetarily tangible benefits were to provide the then unspecified basis of the entire economic formulation, justification and evaluation of the project even though no formulae were spelled out. In fact, the current problems of the Water Resources Council focus, in part, around this same fundamental question, that is, how to assess intangibles and meaningfully include them in any quantitative balance sheet.

The "Proposed Practices for Economic Analysis of the River Basin Projects" which became known as the Green Book, was issued in 1950 by the Sub-committee on Benefits and Costs (1950) of the Federal Interagency River Basin Committee. This informal Committee succeeded in preventing threats of Congressional interference with established Executive Branch activities. The procedures established by the Green Book (and later modified) are those which NEPA now imposes, yet many of the water resources guidelines led to NEPA's enactment. Secretary Udall was influential in both.

The Green Book was given the force of law through Circular A-47 of the Bureau of the Budget in 1950. This document spelled out in considerable detail how to apply the benefit-cost analysis in keeping with the spirit of the 1936 Omnibus Flood Control Act charge. The controversies raised and laid to rest by this document are discussed at length by Eckstein (1958).

Circular A-47 and the Green Book were superceded in 1962 when President Kennedy directed the Departments of the Executive Branch to prepare projects in accordance with guidelines set forth by the President's Water Resources Council (not to be confused with the Council created by the 1965 Water Resources Planning Act) which was established by President Eisenhower in 1958. Senate Document No. 97, as it is known, declared that Federally-sponsored water and related land resources projects would be evaluated from the standpoints of i) national economic and regional development; ii) proper stewardship, and iii) well-being of people, and that the latter would be "the overriding determinant in considering the best use of water and related land resources"(President's Water Resources Council, 1962). Steward Udall's influence is evident in this document, and it furthered the broadening of goals and more realistic financial evaluations that commenced with the 1958 revision of the Green Book. Neither the latter nor S. D. 97 (and its 1964 Supplement and 1968 Ammendment) were extensively used, however, since the "No New Starts" policy of the Eisenhower administration persisted into the 1960's.

Under the authority of the Water Resources Planning Act (70 Stat 244) of 1965, the Water Resources Council's Task Force is-

11

sued *Procedures for Evaluation of Water and Related Land Resource Projects* in 1969 for consideration before adoption. This proposal recommended that the new guidelines have, as their objectives, i) national income, ii) regional development, and iii) environmental quality. Presumably, the well-being of the people was held to be an implicit underpinning of these three goals, but the national, regional, and local "scales" of impact of the proposed project are specifically identified for the first time. However, the question of how each is to be relatively weighted is omitted. The Water Resources Council held hearings on these proposed principles and standards which emanated from the Task Force Report, and issued a summary of hearings comments (Water Resources Council, 1972). Appropriate revision and adoption has now been completed (Water Resources Council, 1973). These proposed principles and standards are specifically related to NEPA.

The enactment of NEPA may be thought of, too, as the most recent in a long line of (unplanned) steps in the control of the Executive Branch agencies by the Congress. Indeed, NEPA may be an essential step, ensuring full disclosure and public information and participation, on the way toward implementation of the Hoover Commission's recommendation that all natural resource agencies be located under one roof.

Finally, the specific history of NEPA enacted in the waning days of the 1969 session of the 91st Congress is traced in detail by Anderson (1973).

Environmental Crises

Serious air pollution events in the United States and England have given strong impetus to the need for an effective program of environmental quality and have provided the opportunity to see the link between air, soil, and water pollution as well as problems of resources management, generally.

Serious pollution - environmental degradation - episodes and situations have been increasing in frequency and magnitude during the growth of the industrial world. This increasingly unhealthy state of affairs has given strong public support to the need for an effective program for environmental management. The various pollution problems are quite different in their noticability and permanance. Air pollution problems, which have a history that is documented back to the 18th Century and which probably plagued even the cave man, provide a case in point.

Air pollution episodes, as they are called, are transitory in nature, that is, they come and go with the weather, but cannot be ignored when they strike. They can be deadly. The famous London black fog hung over that City for four days, and killed 4,000 people. That particular episode triggered public action and legislation which resulted in the clearing of the London atmosphere. Although the U.S. had its share of such episodes (Donora, Pa., 1948; New York, 1966) none have been as striking as the London fog. Of more concern has been the gradual degradation of the atmosphere of the entire U.S. by the automobile (Esposito, 1970). This national-scale air pollution is noticable and is not escapable: it is everywhere. The public awareness of this situation has probably been important in the acceptance of NEPA and automobile emission standards.

The Dust Bowl of the 30's led directly to the formation of the Soil Conservation (originally Erosion) Service (and other agencies), and the adoption of widespread soil conservation practices. The linking of soil and vegetation conservation was underway, and awaited the final connection with human welfare through water pollution and aquatic-based food chains.

13

The pollution of our waterways and bodies of water is of a slightly different nature: the destruction of the aquatic ecosystem is slow and the destruction, once wrought, is even slower to repair. The scattered documentation and the importance of pollution of water and food chains, was drawn together in *Silent Spring* by Rachael Carson in 1962. That book finally launched the Environmental Era of the 60's. Gradual deterioration of water was observed in estuarine ecosystems, with the loss of commercial shell fisheries, fish kills along the Mississippi, the gross pollution of Lake Erie, and other lakes, and the simultaneous recognition of the impact of concentration of DDT throughout the aquatic food chains.

These environmental crises contributed to the public's awareness of the problem and led in part, to NEPA.

The Content of NEPA

NEPA consists of both a statement of national environmental policy and a provision for an effecting mechanism. Title I of the Act declares the policy in spirit:

> The Congress, recognizing the profound impact of man's activity on the interrelations of all components of the natural environment, ... declares that it is the continuing policy of the Federal Government ... to create and maintain conditions under which man and nature can exist in productive harmony ...

It should be pointed out that this does not create in the citizens of the United States a substantive right to some specified condition of the environment, for the Act utilizes the word "should" rather than "shall" with respect to individual rights to a healthful environment and attendant responsibilities. Section 102 declares that all units of the federal Government shall interpret and administer their activities in light of Section 101 and, in the best-known part of the Act, states:

> (2) all agencies of the Federal Government shall ...(C) include in every recommendation or report on proposals for legislation and other major Federal actions significantly affecting the quality of the human environment, a detailed statement by the responsible official on ...
> (i) the environmental impact of the proposed action,
> (ii) any adverse environmental effects...,
> (iii) alternatives to the proposed action,
> (iv) the relationship between local short-term uses and long-term productivity, and
> (v) any irreversible and irretrievable commitments of resources ...

Further Sections of the Title cover broad details of responsibility and implementation, as well as responsibility for review of decisions and statements. The Environmental Impact Statement, often referred to simply as a "102 statement," is at once the implementation of the policy stated in Section 101 and the evidence that that policy is being lived up to (Goldsmith, 1973). We further believe that it simultaneously becomes the descriptor of the environment, the action, and the impact. *Thus, if accomplished with constructive thoughtfulness, the 102 statement can be a tool of the resource manager and planner, the communications link between professional and lay public, and the basis for sound decision-making, regardless of where that responsibility lies.*

Title II of the Act provides for the establishment of a Council on Environmental Quality to advise the President on matters pertaining to the environment, to recommend legislation, and to generally oversee the workings of all that NEPA implements. The Council consists of three members, appointed by the President and with the advice and consent of the Senate, the chairman of which shall also serve as Director of the Office of Environmental Quality

established by Title II of the Water Quality Improvement Act of
1970 (PL 91-224) and often cited as the Environmental Quality
Improvement Act of 1970 (not to be confused with NEPA). The
Secretary to the Council who, in effect, runs the Office, is
appointed by the Council and approved by the President.

The Council and Office are arranged as shown in Figure 1.

Figure 1. Organization Chart of the Council on Environmental Quality

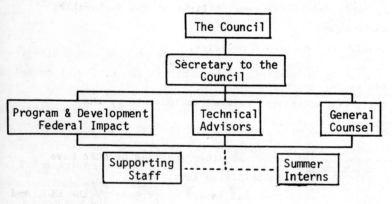

Note that there is no formal link between the Council or Office
on Environmental Quality and the Environmental Protection Agency
(EPA) which was established as an independent agency in the
Executive Branch by Reorganization Plan 3 of 1970. EPA combines,
under one roof, most of the regulatory and enforcement offices
of several agencies which previously were scattered both geographically and administratively. EPA also does research and, for a

more complete discussion of the responsibilities and functions
of EPA as well as the other Federal agencies charged with environmental concerns, see Chapter IV.

The Council has the following responsibilities as detailed
in Section 204:

i)   to assist and advise the President in the preparation of
       the report required in Section 201,
ii)   to compile and submit to the President studies relating
       to virtually any and all matters which concern NEPA,
       and to gather such information,
iii)   to review existing programs in light of the declaration
       of policy,
iv)   to develop and recommend policies,
v)   to document changes in the environment,
vii)   to report to the President, and
viii) to carry out additional related assignments by the
       President, as requested.

Interpretation of these and other sections of NEPA have
led to two additional responsibilities involving;

ix)   the review of environmental impact statements by the CEQ, and
x)   the establishment of guidelines for their preparation,
       which appeared officially on April 23, 1971, (CEQ, 1971),
       and which were revised August 1, 1973, (see Appendix B).

To further a comprehensive attack on all environmental matters,
CEQ has, with authority of Executive Order 11514 (March 5, 1970),
created advisory committees, including ones dealing with;

xi)   how existing tax structure affects environmental quality,
xii)   law, and
xiii) development of a non-polluting automobile

17

The Council has established and revised the guidelines for the preparation and review of 102 statements and, having been published in the Federal Register, these have the force of law. The revised guidelines are abstracted as follows (For complete guidelines, see Appendix).

1) *Purpose:* to effect policy declaration of NEPA;

2) *Policy:* condensation of Title I of NEPA;

3) *Agency and OMB Procedures:* all agencies will file with CEQ their proposals for precisely how they intend to implement the CEQ guidelines;

4) *Federal agencies included:* Section 102(2)C of the Act applies to all agencies of the Federal Government ... unless existing law ... expressly prohibits or makes compliance "impossible";

5) *Actions included:*

   a) recommendations or favorable reports relating to legislation including requests for appropriations, regardless of proposal's source;

   b) new and continuing projects and program activities, and

   c) the making, modification, or establishment of regulations, rules, procedure, and policy;

6) *Identifying Major Actions Significantly Affecting the Environment*

   a) The term "Major Actions Significantly Affecting the Environment: is to be construed by agencies with a view to the overall, cumulative impact of the proposed action. This includes, but is not limited to, actions that are localized in their impact, that are likely to be highly controversial and (those actions) that, when added to other smaller actions, result in cumulatively considerable impacts;

   b) "Significant Effects" also include secondary effects;

18

limitation of beneficial uses, particularly on long-
term vs. short-term considerations;

7. *Procedures for Preparing Draft Environmental Statements; Hearings:*

 a) Agencies should (i) maintain a list of actions for which 102 statements are being prepared (ii) revise the list regularly (iii) make the list public;

 b) Each 102 statement shall be circulated in draft form as early as possible;

 c) If more than one Federal agency is involved, only one statement is required;

 d) The agency should make its own evaluation of the environmental issues;

 e) Agency Guidelines should include provision for public hearings on proposed actions, whenever appropriate;

8) *Content of Environmental Statements:*

 The points to be covered are enumerated, as they are worded in Section 102(2) of NEPA.

9) *Review of Draft 102 Statements by appropriate Federal, State, and Local Agencies and by the Public:*

 a) Federal Review; - obtain comments from federal agencies with jurisdiction by law or special expertise in the area of the proposed action;

 b) E.P.A. review under Clean Air Act - (as stated under Section 309 of Clean Air Act);

 c) State and Local Review - A current listing of clearing-houses which provide views of state and local environmental agencies is issued periodically by the Office of Management and Budget:

10) *Preparation and Circulation of Final 102 Statements:*

 Final statements, with comments from the draft statement attached, shall be sent to all federal, state, and local agencies and private organizations that made substantive

requesting a copy);

11) *Distribution of Statements to C.E.Q.:*
   a) Ten (10) copies of all draft statements at least
      90 days prior to any administrative action and ten
      (10) copies of all submitted comments and final
      statement at least 30 days prior to the proposed
      administrative action. Also, there are provisions
      for special cases, situations involving congressional
      action, and emergencies;

12) *Legislative Actions:* A final 102 statement should be
    available to the Congress and the Public on proposals
    for legislation to which 102(2)C applies. In some cases,
    a draft statement will suffice;

13) *Application of 102(2)C Procedure to Existing Projects and
    Programs:* NEPA applies to these "even though they arise
    from projects or programs initiated prior to enactment
    of the Act on 1/1/70";

14) *Supplementary Guidelines, Evaluations of Procedures:* This
    is provision for revision and further specification of
    details.

In summary, NEPA rapidly and effectively brought about the
means for self-examination of the environmental impact which
would result from federal actions. However, the simple wording
of NEPA, including such words as "detailed," "to the fullest
extent possible," "significant impact," "at the earliest feasible
time," and even "ecological systems" and "environment," to
mention a few, has left open the door to serious questioning of
the intent of Congress, and many extensive court conflicts have
ensued as a direct result of this wording and were, in fact,
responsible for the revision of the original guidelines.

The courts have broadly applied and extended both the intent and the spirit of NEPA, as well as related pre-NEPA court decisions and legislation. There are several pre-NEPA court decisions of relevance: the intent of the Federal Power Act regarding comprehensive plans was upheld in *Scenic Hudson Preservation Conference v. FPC* (354 F2d 608) in 1965 when the Court determined that the Federal Power Commission had failed to consider Storm King's (a proposed pumped-storage project) potential adverse scenic impact on the River, that is, according to the Council on Environmental Quality·(1971) "the Second Circuit Court held that 'recreational purposes' includes conservation of natural resources and maintenance of natural beauty." The precedent established in Storm King was upheld in 1967 in the decision concerning the construction of the High Mountain Sheep Dam on the Snake River (*Udall v. FPC*, 387 US 428). Other considerations were added, however, including whether the power development should be public or private and whether any dam should be built, considering the public interest in recreation and fisheries concerns on the Snake.

Although NEPA was not specifically under consideration, the decision in *Zabel v. Tabb* (430 F2d 199, 1970; cert. denied 39 USLW 3360, 1971) established that environmental quality would be a reasonable input in the decision-making process even where the purpose of permit review was not environmental quality. Thus, the decision of the Corps of Engineers to deny a permit for a trailer park requiring fill, and thereby coming under control of navigable waterways on ecological grounds was not beyond that agency's jurisdiction and the implication is that every Federal agency shall consider ecological factors regardless of whether the primary concern is ecological.

statutes of relevance: The first is the Administrative Procedures Act (APA) of 1946 (60 Stat 237, as amended 5 USC 551, *et. seq.*) which establishes formal procedures for adjudication and rulemaking. Federal agencies must appraise anyone who chooses to follow the development of a proposed action 1) through the process of holding a hearing similar to a trial with subsequent statement summarizing testimony, findings, conclusions, and decisions available for court review and action (adjudication), or 2) through publication in the Federal Register when formulating, amending, or repealing a rule (rulemaking). With publication as required in the Federal Register, the rule obtains the force of law, as is the case, for example, with Guidelines established by the Council on Environmental Quality.

The second statute is the Freedom of Information Act (8 Stat 54) of 1967 which provides that each agency of the Federal government shall make available to the public descriptions of its organizations, offices, and information depositories; statements of its functional methods; rules of procedures, and substantive rules, policies, interpretations, and applications, as well as final opinions. Items from the above not listed in the Federal Register, and administrative manuals and instructions whenever such "affects a member of the Public" are also to be included. There are specific exclusions relating to national defense, current litigation, matters of private concern, and the like. The intent of the Act, however, is clear, and it may be invoked to persuade an agency to disclose its activities when not, essentially, of some sensitive nature and in the public interest.

With these two Acts, and numerous decisions both before and since enactment of NEPA, the citizen is finding that his right to participate in governmental activities is more of a reality than ever before. However, participation by the public outside of the above formal channels depends upon an individual's interest and initiative in getting to and participating in hearings.

Participation by the public in court proceedings has been limited to individuals who had "standing" in court, that is, could show conclusively that, by action of the agency, he would be injured in person or property, that he was in fact aggrieved. This allowed only a rather limited amount of "public" participation. In fact, the cards were often stacked against the private citizen who had to battle payrolled professionals, legal consultants, testimony of agency personnel, agency funds to carry on expensive litigation, and wide-ranging expertise. To do battle effectively, the individual must shoulder equal effort on his own, not to mention court costs, should he lose. In addition, the citizen must, if he is to be recognized in court (even with standing) participate in all administrative steps and go through all administrative channels available to him in the decision-making process. Further, if he is to successfully prosecute pollution under the nuisance laws, he must also come into court "with clean hands," that is, he must in no way be guilty of the same offense which he is attempting to prosecute.

With the passage of NEPA, some of the problems which the frustrated citizen has faced in the past are being resolved. With several successes to encourage them, both the individual and those organizations working in his behalf (notably Environmental Defense Fund, Natural Resources Defense Council, National Wildlife Federation, and The Sierra Club) are seeking new levels of responsible participation in decisions that affect the environment. In the early post-NEPA years, litigation had been characterized as being concerned with substantive matters as well as procedural concerns where agencies have tried to end-run NEPA and either not prepare 102 statements at all or prepare inadequate ones. Some of these constructive court battles have been vociferously degraded under the generalized and derogatory heading "obstructionist." It has been claimed, as a consequence, that the public is having a field day with their new-found legal weapon, but it is also true that the agencies are interested in finding out precisely what it is that they are required to do. When the smoke clears, the way should be cleared, too, to make constructive use of the 102 statement.

The courts have dealt directly with questions of standing, procedures, and interpretation of the definable words cited above in such a manner as to extend the intent and spirit of NEPA. It has taken the courts about three years to "establish the basic trends of interpretation..." (Resources for the Future, 1973). By May, 1972, 2933 environmental impact statements were filed with the Council on Environmental Quality (1972). As of August 1, 1973, a total of 419 cases involving impact statements, or the absence thereof, had been brought before the courts. From these, a few involve precedents and are summarized as follows:

The question of standing was ruled on in the case of Mineral King (*Sierra Club v. Morton*, 433 F2d 24, 1970) to be inviolate and shall remain so unless the appeal produces a reversal of the 9th Circuit Court decision. On the other hand, the Supreme Court has found that the injury need not be economic in nature, but may be aesthetic, conservational, or recreational (*Data Processing Service v. Camp*, 397 US 150, 1970). It would certainly seem that the Court will have to put some limit on citizens' rights in court with regard to NEPA to preclude a log jam of suits where no criteria other than being citizens is required, yet allowing perhaps some time in the future, for the violation of an individual's substantive right to a healthful environment to be sufficient for standing. It should also be pointed out that once the citizen has attained standing under current court practice, any subject relevant to the case, i.e., to the proposed action, may be the subject of litigatory proceedings, regardless of whether they comprise the primary cause of injury in fact.

The question of interpretation of the word "detailed" was dealt with in *Calvert Cliffs' Coordinating Committee, Inc. v. AEC* (449 F2d 1109, 1119, D.C. Cir. 1971) when the court held that the Atomic Energy Commission must, under NEPA, consider *all* aspects of environmental quality, not just radiological health according to that agency's organic act. In spite of this, the courts have still not defined a limit on the amount of detail, just the extent of coverage, and probably will not do so until it has a chance to consider a definitive project with a substantial amount of detail in its environmental impact statement which is questioned on merits. The guidelines and checklists provided by the Council on Environmental Quality are still just guidelines, not forms with so much space to be filled up. We feel, as is spelled out in detail below, that there can be no set limit and, in fact, *the environmental impact statement must reflect the environment being impacted, and therefore represent that environment to the extent that detail about it is known,* thus uniquely limiting the detail of the statement itself. Note that the Court further held that rules of the AEC which did not require a detailed statement in an *uncontested* licensing procedure did not comply with Section 102(2).

In an attempt to bypass the provision in NEPA that Section 102(2)C apply even to projects underway, the Corps of Engineers received a setback when challenged by Environmental Defense Fund (EDF) in the Gilham Dam proposal on the Arkansas River (*EDF v. Corps of Engineers*, 325 F. Supp 728, 1971). Construction of the dam was finally allowed to proceed, but only after preparation of the impact statement (EDF, 1973). This case is also important because the question of standing arose, too: the court held that Section 101 did not create a substantive right in the public at large, but that EDF did have standing on the basis that NEPA *did* create in the people a substantive right to have the *procedures* adhered to and it is on this basis that EDF obtained access to the court. The outcome, of course, is that the Corps had to prepare a 102 statement on the Gilham Dam proposal and, presumably, must also do so on any and all projects which have been authorized for as much as thirty years as part of more or less comprehensive river basin plans, but which have not been constructed or had funds appropriated, since to complete the works would constitute a "major" action. The precedent may be applied to other agencies as well.

The extent to which the project-sponsoring agency must include review comments was of secondary concern in the Amchitka Decision (*Committee for Nuclear Responsibility v. Seaborg*, 3 ERC 1126, 315 F. Supp. 1205, 1971) -- the primary one being the attempt to halt nuclear weapons testing -- for the Court held that the AEC had not, and indeed must, include opponents' views in their summarization of comments on the draft statement.

The term "major action" required definition: What constitutes a Federal action is spelled out in the CEQ Guidelines (see above) but one action not covered therein was handled in *National Helium Corporation v. Morton* (326 F. Supp. 151, 1971) when the government saw fit to cancel a contract for the purchase of helium from the plaintiff. In the event of cancellation, the helium would be released to the atmosphere and the notice of cancellation was not accompanied by a 102 statement on the environmental impact of such an "action." The court held that it should be.

Although the CEQ Guidelines specify that the 102 statement will be prepared by the responsible official, that is, the one on whose shoulders the responsibility for the action's decision rests, the Federal Power Commission had attempted to utilize the environmental impact statement prepared by the Power Authority of the State of New York. The Power Authority had applied for a license for a power line right-of-way from a pumped-storage project in the Schoharie Valley: the Court held that the FPC practice was in violation of the spirit of NEPA and that each agency must prepare its *own* statement (*Greene County Planning Board, et al, v. Federal Power Commission,* 455 FED. REP. 412, 1972). It is expected, again, that this precedent-setting case will be extended to include all license and permitting type of actions on the part of Federal regulatory agencies. This important decision places the burden of compliance with Section 102(2)C squarely on the Federal agencies, although there is at present no restriction on contracting with private consultant firms for statement preparation. An important exception is the Federal Highway Administration which, through rigid guidelines and close supervision, routinely accepts EIS' of State Departments of Transportation as their own.

What constitutes an alternative to an action cannot, perhaps, ever be spelled out for all cases, but the extent to which the sponsoring agency must be concerned about environmental quality in keeping with Section 101 of the Act is indicated by the decision in *Natural Resources Defense Council, Inc., v. Morton* (3 ERC 1558, 1972): the Court held that the Department of the Interior, while considering granting a permit for offshore oil leases must consider, as a *reasonable* alternative, modifying the oil import quotas, but not producing power by solar radiation. Again, this is another important decision for it forces the agency to consider alternatives beyond its own "boundaries."

Finally, the question of substantive rights of the American public remain undecided and, in fact, may not be decided under NEPA. Nevertheless, it may come to pass that an agency completely complies with NEPA and, despite its expert judgment, makes the "wrong" decision. Under such a predicament, the courts will be asked to step in and examine the merits of the action in question and thereby decide the substantive matter more definitively. More specifically, the courts may be asked to rule on what constitutes "productive harmony" and other less-than-perfectly defined terms of Section 101.

In this initial post-NEPA period, we see the public flexing its new-found muscle while, at the same time, the government is exploring its legal limits and, as a consequence of non-coincidence of short-term goals associated with each group, conflicts will continue. They should diminish, however, as both groups find they are seeking the same long-term goal of responsible resource management simultaneously with maintenance of environmental quality. Through the National Environmental Policy Act, the difficult job can be accomplished.

Environmental impact can be understood only when the environment and its supporting and dependent ecosystems are understood and defined. One of the major problems in environmental impact analysis is representing, in comprehensive and relevant form, the complex ecosystem-environment interaction. Other problem areas to be treated in this chapter concern the nature of the action and its impact and the place of economic or benefit-cost analysis.

The Environment

Quite often there is little difficulty in determining what is environment -- particularly when man's senses are involved. Most people would respond to the question "What environmental impact?" with "air pollution, noise, water pollution, etc." All these answers are correct since air, water, and soil make up the fabric of the environment, but they shed little light on the total impact of these environmental changes. The answers are a manifestation of man's concern first with environmental changes which affect his senses and those systems on which he is dependent, and secondly, with those systems on which he presupposes no dependence. The ambient air quality standards created by the Clean Air Act (42 USC 1857b 1 Supp. III, 1967) are a reflection of this attitude since the primary air quality standards are based on health while secondary air quality standards are based on property.

The environment, according to the dictionary, is all that surrounds an object being environed. According to Hawley (1973) ". . . The environment is a generic concept for whatever is external to and potentially influential upon a unit under study . . . Thus, the environment is composed of everything which is external to a particular unit of interest. For environmental impact analysis the unit of interest is an ecosystem. Before developing concepts necessary for an environmental impact analysis, then, the concept of ecosystem must be developed.

The term "system" is used to describe an entity which has the properties listed below (Strahler and Strahler, 1973). These properties apply specifically to open systems, that is, systems which are open to the flow of energy and matter across their boundaries. These open systems have:

1. boundaries, real or arbitrary
2. inputs and outputs of energy and matter across the boundary and transport and transformation of energy and matter within the system
3. storage of both energy and matter within the system
4. a state of dynamic equilibrium with inputs equal to outputs
5. an ability to come to a new dynamic equilibrium when inputs and outputs are changed
6. a sensitivity to changes in input and output which is related directly to the amount of storage within the system
7. destruction of the system if inputs of energy or matter or both are eliminated

The environment which surrounds a system controls the system through the control of energy and matter flow between and within the systems. The first problem, then, is the definition of the system being impacted.

Definition of the Ecosystem

The ecosystem has been defined by Schultz (1961) as an integrated organization of biological entities and physical factors while Lindeman (1955) defines an ecosystem as a "system composed of physical - chemical - biological processes active within a space

time unit of any magnitude." The basic idea is that an ecosystem
is a system which contains *living* material. To this basic idea
we add the general properties of systems (listed above) to arrive
at a more practical system of ecosystem identification. First,
there is the *boundary* of the system. This boundary can be natural
(lake, forest stand) or arbitrary (township, lot) depending upon
the needs of the analysis and the nature of the environmental
change. Determination of the boundary suitable to the problem
at hand is not always easy. As was mentioned above, many of our
ideas concerning environmental impact revolve around man and his
health. However, this view of environmental change will tell you
very little about the impact of the change on natural ecosystems
such as lakes, fields, forests. In cities, for instance, we
are more concerned for man's environment within the city rather
than the city environment.

In order to determine the environment of one system it may
be necessary to determine the operation of a larger system which
is providing, partially, the environment for the included system.
An environmental impact may disrupt the operation of the larger
system and thus provide a secondary change in the environment
at the second level.

Odum (1971) points out that the earth is an ecosystem which
contains many spatial subdivisions; each of these subdivisions
is also a system. These systems may exist side by side, may be
nested, and may or may not be connected in time. In addition,
for the purposes of analysis, it may be necessary to consider
some ecosystems as being overlapping. Figure 2 shows these
ideas diagramatically. It is evident from this figure that the
environment for the forest floor ecosystem is determined in
large measure by the functioning of the forest ecosystem since
this larger system modifies and warps the air, water and soil
fabric of the environment.

Figure 2.--Some ecosystem boundaries.

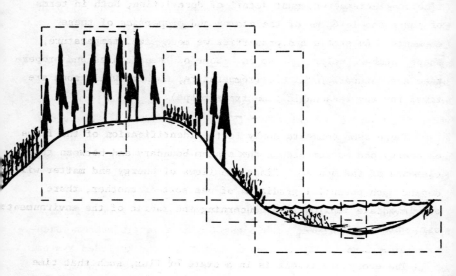

Forest

Edge

vegetation

Lake

opening

soil

epilimnion

hypolimnion

Inclusive   *Overlapping*   *Exclusive*

Nested

Secondly, the *elements* or *parts* of the ecosystem must be identified and catalogued. The extent to which the parts of the ecosystem must be defined and described will depend on the extent to which an impact can be identified downward on a scale of fewer and fewer objects. As need of detail of impact identification increases so must detail of description, both in terms of parts and in terms of the *states* and *properties* of these elements. By states and properties we mean size, temperature, shape, number, color, and so on. Some of these states and properties are naturally variable (temperature, number) while some are fixed for any reasonable time frame (shape).

These same comments apply to the identification of the flows of energy and matter across the system boundary and between the elements of the system. Since the flows of energy and matter will depend upon potential gradients of one sort or another, there are immediate implications concerning the fabric of the environment: air, water, and soil.

The ecosystem itself is in a state of flux, such that time becomes the vital part of the definition of the ecosystem. "The ecosystem ... is considered to be ... interacting with the physical environment so that a flow of energy leads to characteristic trophic structure and material cycles within the system." Odum (1969) thus defines ecological succession as:

> i) an orderly process of community development that is reasonably directional and, therefore, predictable.
> ii) it results from modification of the physical environment by the community ... and
> iii) it culminates in a stabilized ecosystem in which maximum biomass (or high information content) and symbiotic function between organisms are maintained per unit of energy flow.

The time-state of the ecosystem must be in reference to other ecosystems and the environment of that ecosystem, as well as to its own "orderly process of community development."

Ecosystems may be classified in a variety of ways; in fact, this is the essential first step in preparing an environmental impact statement. The external characteristics of the ecosystem permit classification, primarily on the basis of the definition of the boundary or boundaries, thus allowing, for descriptive purposes, one ecosystem to be exclusively defined and isolated from any other ecosystem. The constitution and arrangement of internal characteristics such as elements, states, and relationships provide another basis for classification of ecosystems, along with categorization of their time-states or flow of energy and material within or across boundaries. Ecosystems may also be classified on the basis of their behavior, function or reaction to impact.

For purposes of environmental impact analysis the classification of the ecosystem should be orchestrated so as to reflect the differentiation needed to best illustrate the intensity and extent of the impact, that is, the effect of the action on the environment.

The Action

The understanding of an impact also requires that the nature of the action being taken be considered. Actions may be classified according to their *stage, dynamics, repeatability,* and *status* (Table 2).

Stage refers to whether the action is under *construction* or in full *operation*. Certain actions may not have a construction stage at all, but may merely be in the process of implementation, as is the case with promulgation of standards.

Table 2. Categories of Action

Category	Types of Action
Stage	*Construction / Operation*
Dynamics	*Active / Passive*
Repeatability	*Occurring Once / Recurring*
Status	*Presence / Effect of Presence Itself*

Table 3. Categories of Impact

Category	Types of Impact	
Class	*aesthetic*	*non-aesthetic*
Feedback	*positive*	*negative*
Immediacy	*direct*	*indirect*
Importance	*high*	*low*
Magnitude	*large*	*small*
Probability	*high*	*low*
Quantification	*measurable*	*unmeasurable*

Dynamics of an action involves whether the action is *active* such as a physical, chemical, or biological instrusion on the environment or *passive*, for example, the requirement of NEPA that calls for consideration of the lack of action as one alternative, for it, too, has an impact. However, there are also specific actions that are passive in nature. For example, the creation of Wilderness Areas, or restrictive standards, both of which are do-nothing policies.

Repeatability of the action simply describes whether the action is a *one-shot* occurrence or is *recurring*. The construction stage is usually one-shot, but the operation may involve recurring impacts. Maintenance of a facility should be considered under recurring actions, along with operation.

Status refers to the fact that an action may be considered simply as a *presence*, for example, the direct and indirect impacts caused by a road, or as the *effect* of that presence, for example, repeated use of the road by vehicles.

The Impact
Classification

Owing to the large number of variables in both the environment and the action, succinct definition of impact categorization is difficult, at best. We identify at least seven classes of impacts, some or all of which may be of concern in the impact statement. These are identified in Table 3. Several of these types represent ends of a spectrum for the category rather than mutually exclusive or opposite conditions.

In the case of impact *class*, it should be easy to ascertain whether or not the impact is disruptive of the ecosystem, that is, non-aesthetic (Jowett, 1972). Any given impact may involve both classes of impact, but the ones that are most difficult to assess are those which are purely aesthetic in nature and which, being largely subjective, are interpreted differently by different individuals.

A positive *feedback* impact is one in which the impact grows as a result of the effect of the action, whereas a negative one diminishes or is maintained at a constant level in time.

Variation in space, as opposed to time, is accounted for by the *immediacy* of the impact. A direct impact is one in which the action itself imposes the environmental intrusion or aesthetic degradation; whereas an indirect impact is one in which the impact is caused by an induced effect. Thus, a road has both direct and indirect impacts: in the first instance, local drainage ways are modified by blocking streams to a greater or lesser extent. An indirect effect would be that the relocation of the waterways and increased surface runoff may result in downstream flooding which previously did not exist. Another example of indirect impact is the air and noise pollution which results from the use of the road by motor vehicles (these would be direct impacts of the ve-hicles). In other words, one impact of an action may be to induce another action, with its attendant impacts. We consider the latter to be indirect impacts of the former.

The *importance* (and *magnitude*) of the impact is identified by Leopold, *et al* (1971) on scales of 1 to 10, with high numbers indicating greater importance and magnitude. Thus, it is possible to have an impact of high magnitude, but of relatively little consequence, therefore of low import. Conversely, it is also possible to have a rather minor impact in terms of magnitude, yet with considerable ramifications, thus high import.

The *probability* of an impact occurring is closely related
to both magnitude and importance. That is, an impact which has
both a large magnitude and a high importance but with a low
probability would be quite different from a low importance and
magnitude, but high probability-of-occurrence, impact, Thus,
the impact of an accident at a nuclear power plant would be of
very high importance and magnitude, but of relatively low
probability in contrast to storm-induced bypassing of a municipal
sewage treatment plant. The latter, which is of only moderate
importance, magnitude, and probability requires much more attention
in environmental impact statements. Of course, the occurrence
of low importance-magnitude-probability impacts, like the other
extreme, needs only mere documentation to establish the fact that
these aspects have been considered.

Quantification, particularly of the middle-ground importance/
magnitude/probability impact, is where controversy finds sustenance.
It is in this area of impact analysis that the predictive ability
of the ecosystem models is of prime importance. These models require
numerical data.

Evaluation of the impact is the proper summarization of these
several categories of ecosystem, action, and impact.

Evaluation

Evaluation of environmental impact of an action has tradition-
ally been limited to application of benefit-cost analysis to the
readily-measured engineering aspects of the program or project
that constitutes the action (Generally, see Eckstein, 1958; and
Howe, 1971). As specified in the Green Book, principles of
application of the benefit-cost analysis were to be adopted by
all major Federal agencies involved in river basin planning in
the Departments of Agriculture; Commerce; Health, Education and

Welfare; Interior, and Labor; the Federal Power Commission, and the Corps of Engineers. These principles included operational principles for consideration of alternatives, points of evaluation of goods and services, merits of net-versus maximum benefits, identification of separable segments, and usage of the resultant benefit-cost ratio in determing priorities. Unfortunately, considerable vagueness and ambiguity in the specific statements was the direct result of compromise between the agencies represented on the Subcommittee, and specific agency practice was more detailed, although generally within the overall principles. The Green Book defined relevant terms, and identified several guidelines to be followed to arrive at a comprehensive evaluation of benefits and costs. Though recognizing it as an impossibility, the Green Book recommended that consideration be given to all possible sites, routes, locations, and scales of the project, along with alternative

However, in practice, the Green Book never forced adequate consideration of alternatives as NEPA does, which lack may have been a major factor in the enactment of the NEPA. The same may be said of evaluation of less tangible concerns. Thus, the economic impact of pollution and other environmental impacts have in the past, been considered "social" costs, presumably not subject to evaluation. Recent studies have been directed at closer evaluation of these impacts, and "in general, the studies found that the impact of those pollution control costs that were estimated and examined would not be severe in that they would not seriously threaten the long-run economic viability of the industrial activities examined. However, the estimated impact is not inconsequentia in that there are likely to be measurable impacts both on the economy as a whole and on individual industries" (Anon., 1972).

The Green Book, Senate Document 97, and the current Principles and Standards of the Water Resources Council, discuss at length the problems of determination of interest rates and length of the period of analysis. These aspects are particularly important for water and related land resources projects since they tend to involve long physical lifespans, high initial costs, and fairly high risk of loss of either structure or value of goods and services. Thus, the primary disadvantage to the purely economically based benefit-cost analysis resides in the complex relationship between the percentage of the total project cost which is fixed (first) cost, the length of analysis, the interest rate, and the benefit-cost ratio. In sum, higher values of B/C are associated with low-interest rates, which are incompatible with the long periods of analysis necessary to justify a project with such a high first cost. In effect, raising the interest rate to account for the higher risk associated with longer periods of analysis would discount long-term values more, devalue non-monetary benefits and, obviously, lower the B/C to a point where the project would no longer be economically feasible.

NEPA mandates a broader analysis than was formerly provided by the Green Book and its successors. This is particularly true if one considers that the benefit-cost analysis should be used to evaluate the WRC objective with enhanced National Income Development, whereas the EIS should be used to evaluate the objective of enhanced Quality of the Environment. The process, we believe, is to inventory the environment, describe the action, and to evaluate the impact. That evaluation involves new as well as traditional methods. Some of these include application of natural principles which are especially useful in evaluating impact, matrix formulation, and new concepts.

Observation of several natural principles in the ecosystem and the environment gives rise to some interpretations which are useful in evaluating impacts: 1) The concept of natural dynamic equilibrium was intriguingly-worded by Marsh (1874): "Nature, left undisturbed, so fashions her territory as to give it almost unchanging permanence of form, outline, and proportion, except when shattered by geologic convulsions; and in these comparatively rare cases of derangement, she sets herself at once to repair the superficial damage, and to restore, as nearly as practicable, the former aspect of her dominion." 2) There is a direct relationship between environmental detail and environmental factors which influence that detail, and this is inversely related to magnitude of the ecosystem being described and to man's ability to effect any changes (Black, 1970). 3) The impact of an action usually diminishes at an increasing rate with distance away from the site of the action, but it is possible for the impact to be unexpectedly concentrated at some distance and time from the site of the action (Reitze, 1972). 4) The impact of an action on the environment often results in slow changes that are difficult to assess or even notice during the process of gradual environmental degradation. 5) One or more impacts may have compensating effects on each other, or may induce synergistic responses by reacting with each other or with one or more factors of the environment.

An example of compensating impacts may be found in Onondaga Lake, New York, where the combined effluents of Solvay Process Company's lime and Syracuse's phosphate form sludge which sinks to the bottom, therefore, not polluting the lake's surface waters. A full-scale treatment of the City's sewage, therefore, would constitute an action that would have a severe environmental impact on the Lake. Likewise, so would the closing of the Company.

A synergistic effect is one where the results of two simultaneous actions is not simply additive, but often quite different from the result of either action alone owing to complex interactions Synergistic impacts are common, quite complex, and difficult to identify and predict. One example (Lichtenstein, *et al*, 1973) reports enhanced toxicity of pesticides in the presence of other-wise non-toxic herbicides.

Natural variation of ecosystem, action and impact is mani-fested in the fact that identical actions in different places will not necessarily have constant impact, thus, 1) actions applied at different points in time in relation to ecosystem development may have different results dependent upon conditions existing at that time, 2) an action applied to similar ecosystems with differing environments, may result in varying interactions with environmental factors, 3) actions applied in different sequences may be expected to produce differing results, 4) an action may have a cumulative impact on the environment, such as has been detected in the concentration of DDT upwards in food chains (Wurster and Wingate, 1971).

Two matrix approaches to impact evaluation have been developed. The first entails both ecological description and intricacies of impact variability and interactions and the matrix provides both a checklist for most types of actions and for the many character-istics and conditions of the environment presented in U. S. Geological Survey Circular 645 by Leopold, *et al* (1971).[2/] The suggested procedure conforms with CEQ guidelines relating to "the probable impact of the proposed action on the environment ... by providing a system for the analysis and numerical weighting of probable impacts. This numerical weighting is achieved by establishing the i) *mag-nitude* of the interaction between action and environment condition; and ii) *importance* of the interaction at that particular time and place, as specified in the action proposal.

_____

[2/] This publication is reproduced in the collected readings for this course *Readings in Environmental Impact*, edited by P. E. Black and L. P. Herrington, MSS Information Corporation, 655 Madison Avenue, N.Y., 1974.

assessing these two values. Various ways are proposed in Circular 645 to arrive at a summation of impact magnitude and importance for each interaction between the proposed action and environmental condition, thus providing, directly from the matrix, a collective assessment of those interactions complete with a numerical indication of where the impact is likely to concentrate, spread out, produce compensating effects, etc. Such results are, to a limited extent, quantitative as shown in Circular 645.

The second is referred to as the cause-condition-effect network (Sorenson, 1972) and has been utilized in an intensive study involving resource degradation and multiple use planning by Sorenson (1971) on the California Coast. The format developed is keyed to *uses* (which we have termed action, as in NEPA) that are associated with *causal factors*, though that linkage may not be permanent. In fact, a change in method of use may effect a change in or elimination (or introduction) of a causal factor which, in turn, will have some impact, or change of condition. This impact is termed an *initial condition* which can be grouped or classified as biological, chemical, or physical impacts, or adverse and favorable, or other systems as suggested earlier. *Consequent conditions* are those that "describe the changes induced by the initial conditions that ultimately produce the *effect* or effects." The physical format of the matrix also allows for the display of *corrective actions* which are "physical measures commonly employed to reduce or eliminate the adverse effects", other measures, which are termed *control mechanisms*, including planning, zoning, regulations, etc., and references, "at least one specific reference to each *causal factor-condition-effect* relationship."

difficult to utilize without computer assistance and, even with that modern aid, proper identification of inputs and interpretation of output is essential. We feel that the matrix is a useful tool in the impact evaluation process, but is not a panacea. It provides the perspective needed to relegate the impact to its proper position with regard to the environment as a whole and to other impacts. Properly used, it can provide the skeleton upon which to hang the meat of the decision-making information.

A fresh approach to controlling the degree of environmental impact is proposed, perhaps as a counterbalance to the benefit-cost analysis. This system (Westman and Gifford, 1973) entails rationing of Natural Resource Units (NRU) to each individual so that no single person would degrade a disproportionate share of environmental quality. Specific actions would be worth predetermined numbers of NRUs and, therefore, individuals would be able to make free choices within an overall limit based upon indifference curves not unlike those encountered when making choices on how to allocate financial resources. Aside from public acceptance of such a scheme, the major problem is determination of the NRU-worth of owning a second car, having a child, operating an air conditioner, etc. Implementation of such a plan is way in the future, but if we consider environmental quality as a resource, then its eventual adoption is as logical as the development of a monetary system.

Additional perspective on inter-ecosystem and inter-environment interactions provides a balanced foundation upon which the environmental impact statement can be constructed, thus ecosystems can be viewed as existing on a background fabric of the physical environment and classified according to the generalized pattern of land use (Table 4). The perspective that this model offers is

44

Table 4. Spectrum of land uses on environmental fabric

Variables	Land Use Classification Spectrum					
	Urban	Suburban	Rural	Rangeland	Forest	Alpine
Social Considerations:						
Population Density	highest--lowest					
Use Intensity	highest--lowest					
Political clout	highest--lowest					
Economics						
Costs, $/Acre	highest--lowest					
Revenues, $/Acre	highest--lowest					
Management [a]	user-oriented--------------------------------resource-oriented					fewer
	often single purpose----------multiple uses					
Ecology	subjugated--dominates					

[a] After Clawson (1963)

particularly valuable in understanding that the greatest impact
of a proposed action might be that which creates a land use out
of context or, according to Table 4, simply "out of place." An
example would be a proposal to build a city-like area in the
middle of a wilderness setting, such as is the case with Mineral
King or Big Sky: A proposal of this nature is likely to:
i) create a profound (i.e., both large magnitude and importance)
impact on the ecology of the area and, ii) create a storm of
opposition, notably from preservationists.

We do not mean to imply that either reaction should be al-
together avoided. Foresight of this nature can at least preclude
being caught unawares, or show that otherwise excellent plans
are completely untenable. Another example is the proposal to
keep or create open space in an urban setting, an act which is
guaranteed to raise the ire of the taxpayer (Babcock, 1966).
The model works equally well in the opposite direction, for one
might consider the lesser environmental impact of a park in the
middle of a city, but the modified environment of the city might
have a profound impact on the park, notably on the ability of
trees, for example, to survive. In addition, social and economic
considerations, representing urban conditions, might lead to
anticipation of such problems as vandalism, carbon monoxide
poisoning of plants, or opposition to the park because it is
a non-revenue-producing use of the land. Additionally, other
considerations could be included which then could be observed to
vary in a more or less predictable fashion along the spectrum of
land uses. These would be presented in such a manner that a
particular type of action might be shown to be especially vulner-
able to inducing a major impact. Some considerations which might
be included are: i) air, noise, or water pollution; ii) transportation networks, or iii) zoning regulations.

It is evident that the types of environmental, ecosystem, action, and impact description presented in this section lend themselves to a reasonable representation of the entire environmental impact as well as constituting a core upon which to build a meaningful statement about that impact. Such a statement can at once provide sufficient detail to accurately describe the impact and to meet the legal requirements of NEPA.

EFFECTIVE CONSTRUCTION OF THE IMPACT STATEMENT

Although the principal administrative goal of the preparation of environmental impact statements is to satisfy the legal dicta of NEPA, most of the studies are ones which should be an integral part of sound resources management in any case. Consequently, NEPA is considered to be "cost-effective" (Anderson, 1973). Beyond that, however, we feel that the environmental impact statement can be utilized to uniquely represent the environment being impacted, as well as to describe the action and impact. Therefore, the statement can become a constructive tool of the resource manager.

To be effective, an impact statement must be deductive, concise, utilitarian, and documented. As an illustration, we have included an environmental impact statement in the Appendix, prepared by the firm of which the authors are partners, and we present this and the next chapter in a format which we believe fulfills these requirements.

1. Environmental impact statements are most usefully constructed when they accurately reflect the environment being impacted. To do this, they must build a special case which takes advantage of the natural ecology of the site, distribute the weight of arguments in accordance with their importance in the environment and, finally, use an effective style.

A Special Case

1.1 Take advantage of the natural ecology, unique to the site of the proposed action, to build a special case. This will include unique features of the ecosystem because a case so constructed can be defended on its own merits and generates a positive approach to resources management.

1.11 Unique features of the ecology include several of the sub-units of the ecosystem (described in Chapter II), namely, elements, states of elements, relationships between elements, boundaries, and temporal and spatial proximities.

1.11a physical arrangement of the elements.
For example, their presence or absence
as a usual or unusual condition, or
a particularly unique combination of
elements. Thus, the combination of
wind direction and mountain barriers
to adequate air drainage may be seen
to create a severe air pollution
impact in an area which otherwise might
seem quite safe and logical for such
use of the dissipative capacity of the
atmosphere.

1.11b The state(s) of the element(s) in
question needs to be examined critically,
as well. An example is the discharge
of sewage effluent via a river into
a large lake which also contains a water
supply inlet. Under the prevailing wind
the inlet is kept clear of diffusing
effluent but, under less frequent storm
conditions, when the wind is out of the
south, is engulfed with effluent aug-
mented by storm runoff which adds natural
pollutants by the normal flushing action
of the hydrologic system.

1.11c The nature of the relationships between
the ecosystem elements also may be
unique, as in the case of rapidly-con-
centrating pollutants in a short food
chain (Wurster and Wingate, 1968;
DeLong, *et al*, 1973).

1.11d Boundaries deserve particular consideration here, for they are almost always
unique, are defined as the limits of
the involved ecosystems, and obviously
are of major importance. Thus, Garvey
(1972) presents the example of coupling
and uncoupling between neighboring
ecosystems in order to control pollutants
introduced into the environment by acid
strip mine drainage. The "pollutant"
need not only be "a resource out of place,"
but might be any action, including a
highway through an aesthetically pleasing
rural countryside, or a land use "out
of context" (See Table 4).

49

1.11c The unique proximity of the action to
any of ecosystem characteristics
(1.11a, b, c, d) in time or space
must also be a part of the description.
Such considerations include the order
in which actions are taken, noting
that the impact in all probability
would not be the same if any two actions
were reversed in time or location.

1.12 A case built upon its unique conditions can
be defended on its own merits, because precedents
although they should not be exclusively relied
upon, vary from case to case.

1.12a Precedents for the particular type of
impact may not exist.

1.12b Precedents should not be relied upon
for the opposing view may find extenu-
ating circumstances (that is, opponents
have built a special case).

1.12c Precedents dictate that the sponsor
will always take the same stand which
may, in fact, be undesirable, since
considerations unique to the site
of action can legitimately require
one position in one case and the opposite position under a different set
of conditions.

1.13 The building of a special case assures assumption
of a positive approach to evaluation of ecosystem,
action, and impact, which should lead to reasonable resource use based on informed decisions.

Representing the Environment

1.2 Distribute the weight of the arguments presented in
accordance with their importance in the environment.
This provides the detail to write an effective report,
and precludes reliance on single issues.

1.21 A well-balanced report is indicative of attention given to all relevant details.

1.21a it illustrates first-hand that the
report does, in fact, represent the
ecosystem (1.33a);

1.21b   the reasoned argument, in its proper
perspective, carries its share of
the weight, and will, therefore, not
attract an undue amount of attention,
with attendant disadvantages (1.22);

1.21c   this concept would be applied as a
general state of mind, as well, in
the interest of strengthening weaker
arguments rather than "watering down"
strong arguments.

1.22   An exception is where the action is being
opposed, and there seems to be little doubt
that a basic objective or premise upon which
the action is based can be successfully challenged, as determined by precedent-setting
cases, changing conditions (including regulations and markets) or public attitudes.

Style and Format

1.3   Utilizing a comprehensible and logical style and format,
prepare the statement in a deductive, documented fashion
so that it will, if necessary, stand up in court. This
will enable comprehension by a wide variety of readers,
provide a utilitarian, deductive, and documented format.

1.31   Prepare the statement in such a manner that it
can be understood and used by a wide variety of
readers.

1.31a   Anticipate the vocabulary limits and
capacities of such widely divergent
readers as the lay public, experts in
your and other fields, superiors (who
may have attained their position via
a professional ladder different from
yours), politicians, reporters, and
lawyers (with no significance whatever
to be attached to the order of presentation!).

1.31b   Start with definitions, preferably
included in the text at the first occurrence of the word; don't use a glossary,
a collection of terms limited to a
special field of knowledge or usage, for

it is too demanding upon the reader
to study it out of context merely
in order to comprehend the text, much
less, put it to use.

1.31c   In the process of explaining a process
or technical problem it is not necessary to start "In the beginning..."
but present a reasonable discussion
and then refer the reader who needs
more background to an accepted reference such as a text that is used to
bring students up to a certain level
of understanding.

1.32   This format lends itself to meeting this rather
obvious requirement (1.31) and is suggested as
a format for the detailed environmental impact
statement, to accurately represent both the
generality and complexity of the environment,
yet comprehensible by non-technical readers.

1.32a   The non-technical reader can get the
sense of the arguments by reading the
non-technical expanded outline represented by the headings down to hundredths;
the reporter might use the table of con-
tents (units and tenths) to provide
perspective for a balanced story; the
politician, with a number of decisions
before him, might only refer to the
summary (units only); and the expert
might read the entire, documented text.

1.32b   The generality of the ecosystem can
be presented in simple terms, while the
detailed description can be expounded in the
text, with terms defined, and references
cited.

1.32c   Like the intricate interrelationships
of the natural ecosystem, this format
can be used to "spin a web" by inverse
relationship between perspective and
detail (1.21) and cross-referencing
(1.34a ii).

format can be utilized to create a
series of nested statements commencing
with broad policy declarations and
leading to specific actions on projects
(2.15d). Such a "tier" system may be
particularly useful in accommodating
the large number of statements required
for similar actions (Anderson, 1973).

1.33   The requirements of logic and deduction lend
        themselves quite readily to inclusion in the
        format recommended.

        1.33a   The statement, that is, the report,
                 must display the same organization,
                 detail, and perspective as is observed
                 in the environment. The extent of
                 detail about the environment to be in-
                 cluded can be easily adapted to this
                 format, for the latter is organized
                 in a fashion similar to that of the
                 environment (1.21a).

        1.33b   The statement must be logical from the
                 standpoint of formal logic. While it
                 is not necessary to lay out arguments
                 in all the detail that that discipline
                 entails, it is wise to make use of
                 the following concepts relating to
                 categorical propositions: i) specifi-
                 cation of subject, or exclusivity of
                 definition of the term; ii) quantity,
                 relating to whether the proposition
                 is about "all" or "some" of the items
                 under consideration, and iii) quality,
                 relating to whether the statement is
                 negative or positive. The importance
                 of these properties lies in the ability
                 to make definitive statements, to avoid
                 conflicting testimony, and to properly
                 pose arguments in relation to one another.

        1.33c   The requirements of a statement that
                 is admitted as evidence at trial are
                 the most rigid. Thus, if the environ-
                 mental impact statement is prepared
                 to meet those standards it may preclude
                 court action itself, and the author may
                 avoid having to write several versions
                 for different readers. It will also

herein as being desirable attributes
of a competent environmental impact
statement.

Documentation

1.34　　Documentation, tracing any declaration back to
some recognized authority, is an essential,
integral part of the preparation of the environmental impact statement.

　　1.34a　　At the conclusion of each final declaration of an argument, there should be
documentation in the form of: i) a
reference to literature cited, utilizing some logical, standardized, and
consistent format; ii) a cross-reference
to another part of the report, which
can be easily accomplished in this format (e.g., 1.33a), or iii) a photograph,
illustration, or graph of original data
or whose source can be cited. This
meets the requirements of formal logic,
as well, by presenting arguments in
deductive fashion, that is, from the
whole to the particular (1.33b ii).

　　1.34b　　Proper documentation commences with
selection of the suitable maps and data
of record upon which to build arguments.
Of utmost importance are considerations
of i) applicability in time and space,
that is, the proximity of the site of
data collection to the site under consideration, because a separation of
but a few miles or a few years may
render some data completely irrelevent,
and ii) scale, which is essentially a
problem of sufficient detail. Maps
are of particular importance, for map
preparation procedure might leave out
detail which is needed and masked by
larger considerations.

　　1.34c　　There is a wide variety of sources of
information about the environment,
including topography, soils, climate,

complications and local, regional, and
State agencies may have some of these
sources or have initiated interpretation
thereof. All exhibits including draw-
ings, photographs, graphs, and maps
should show preparer, scale, and source,
as well as date prepared to be fully
admissible as evidence. Finally, it
is required by the Freedom of Information
Act (81 Stat 54) if the preparer is a
Federal employee, and by common courtesy
and in the interest of good communication
otherwise, that the 102 statement include
a list of recipients of copies.

1.35   Logistically, preparation of a statement in this
        format is relatively easy.

        1.35a   Preparing a suitable-size card for each
                point, the text can be prepared step
                by step and the reference to each point
                may be kept on the card's back or lower
                half.

        1.35b   The cards may be lined up, overlapping
                so as to cover reference material, to
                see how well consecutive statements
                fit together at any level of statement
                (e.g., at the units level, tenths, hun-
                dredths, etc.) and how they may be co-
                ordinated with similar indexed sequences
                in other sections.

        1.35c   This system allows flexibility in that
                cards may be easily altered in their
                desired position simply by changing
                its designation rather than retyping
                an entire page.

        1.35d   Similarly, the entire "manuscript" may
                be readily checked for balance by dis-
                playing the cards *en masse*.

        1.35e   By utilizing all the cards on an appro-
                priate carrier in a copying machine,
                a draft may be prepared rapidly, or
                if just the expanded outline or table
                of contents is desired, the appropriate

above, may be sorted out and copied; or a draft may be prepared directly from the cards by a typist.

1.35f   Finally, the preparation of material on cards allows intermittent work periods to be utilized efficiently, and easy insertion of new sections or single point

Whether or not this particular format is followed is not important; it is essential, however, that the basic criteria set forth at the beginning of this chapter obtain. These ensure that readers with varying degrees of time and technical expertise may delve into the complex problems of environmental impact to the limits of their understanding and to whatever extent desired. In addition, the proper balance of depth and perspective necessary for constructive evaluation of environmental impact is achieved. The particular abbreviated, legal style suggested requires that every statement count and be documented, where possible, and thus due diligence is required of the serious reader. Caution is advised, however, in applying this format to all material; we found, for example, that it did not readily lend itself to the subject matter of Chapters I and II. We have presented our original notes of the next Chapter in the suggested format, as well, to show that it is flexible, for the construction of arguments in Chapter IV is somewhat different from that in Chapter III.

2.   Once the environment, action, and impact have been effectively described, environmental impact statements can be beneficially and constructively used in aiding responsible resources management by understanding the administrative structure of organizations within which their use is required by law. At the Federal level, we have discussed at length the interpretation of NEPA in Chapter I. At this point it is necessary to examine the nature of the Federal government insofar as it pertains to resources management. Relationships between the Federal and local levels need to be understood to assure communication of impact evaluation. As legislation is enacted, State and Local government must be examined because many units are initiating NEPA-like legislation. Finally, the role of the citizen must be examined for NEPA has endowed the public with procedural, as well as certain substantive rights to a quality environment.

The Nature of Executive Branch Organizations

2.1   With all Federal agencies operating under the requirements of NEPA, an understanding of their functions and interactions is an aid to both classifying the bewildering array of agencies and to relating positively to the classification of action and impact.

    2.11   A simple listing of the Federal agencies involves units of the twelve Executive Branch departments, commissions, boards, and other more or less permanent organizations (Office of the Federal Register, 1971). The different groups of agencies are shown in Figure 3.

        2.11a   The Executive departments include those of the President, State; Treasury; Defense Justice; Interior; Agriculture; Commerce; Labor; Health, Education and Welfare; Housing and Urban Development; and Transportation, with some agencies having more resource management responsibilities than others. Most of the resource management activity is centered in Interior and Agriculture.

Figure No. 3

THE GOVERNMENT OF THE UNITED STATES

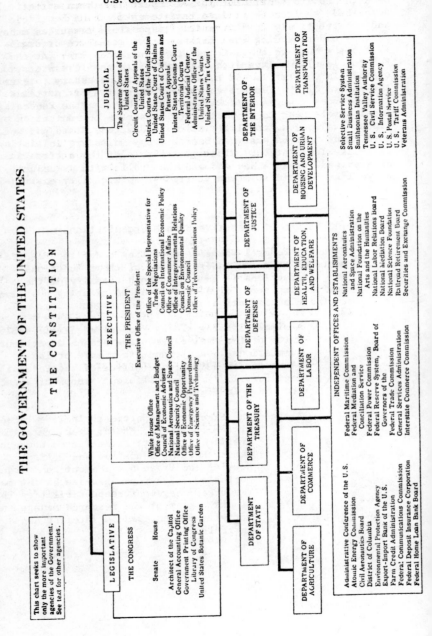

This chart seeks to show only the more important agencies of the Government. See text for other agencies.

THE CONSTITUTION

LEGISLATIVE

THE CONGRESS

Senate   House

Architect of the Capitol
General Accounting Office
Government Printing Office
Library of Congress
United States Botanic Garden

EXECUTIVE

THE PRESIDENT

Executive Office of the President

White House Office
Office of Management and Budget
Council of Economic Advisers
National Aeronautics and Space Council
National Security Council
Office of Economic Opportunity
Office of Emergency Preparedness
Office of Science and Technology

Office of the Special Representative for Trade Negotiations
Council on International Economic Policy
Office of Consumer Affairs
Office of Intergovernmental Relations
Council on Environmental Quality
Domestic Council
Office of Telecommunications Policy

JUDICIAL

The Supreme Court of the United States
Circuit Courts of Appeals of the United States
District Courts of the United States
United States Court of Claims
United States Court of Customs and Patent Appeals
United States Customs Court
Territorial Courts
Federal Judicial Center
Administrative Office of the United States Courts
United States Tax Court

DEPARTMENT OF AGRICULTURE
DEPARTMENT OF COMMERCE
DEPARTMENT OF STATE
DEPARTMENT OF THE TREASURY
DEPARTMENT OF DEFENSE
DEPARTMENT OF HEALTH, EDUCATION, AND WELFARE
DEPARTMENT OF JUSTICE
DEPARTMENT OF THE INTERIOR
DEPARTMENT OF LABOR
DEPARTMENT OF HOUSING AND URBAN DEVELOPMENT
DEPARTMENT OF TRANSPORTATION

INDEPENDENT OFFICES AND ESTABLISHMENTS

Administrative Conference of the U.S.
Atomic Energy Commission
Civil Aeronautics Board
District of Columbia
Environmental Protection Agency
Export-Import Bank of the U.S.
Farm Credit Administration
Federal Communications Commission
Federal Deposit Insurance Corporation
Federal Home Loan Bank Board

Federal Maritime Commission
Federal Mediation and Conciliation Service
Federal Power Commission
Federal Reserve System, Board of Governors of the
Federal Trade Commission
General Services Administration
Interstate Commerce Commission

National Aeronautics and Space Administration
National Foundation on the Arts and the Humanities
National Labor Relations Board
National Mediation Board
National Science Foundation
Railroad Retirement Board
Securities and Exchange Commission

Selective Service System
Small Business Administration
Smithsonian Institution
Tennessee Valley Authority
U.S. Civil Service Commission
U.S. Information Agency
U.S. Postal Service
U.S. Tariff Commission
Veterans Administration

2.11b   The major resource-managing agencies outside the executive department include the Atomic Energy Commission, Council on Environmental Quality, Environmental Protection Agency, Federal Highway Administration, Federal Power Commission, National Water Commission, Office of Emergency Preparedness, Public Land Law Review Commission, Tennessee Valley Authority, and the Water Resources Council.

2.11c   Ever since the first Hoover Commission, there have been repeated attempts to reorganize these sprawling bureauocracies with little success on the part of Congress and somewhat more by Presidential fiat. It is pointed out (Schad, 1968) that much of the reason for lack of Congressional support is due to the committee structure of the Congress which regulates activities, programs, and funds of the several agencies, and the vested interests of Senators and Congressmen in these committees would be diminished simultaneously with department overhauls.

2.12   Classifying the units of the Federal government by function assists analysis of their relations to each other and to NEPA.

    2.12a   The functions recognized are:

        i)   administrative-land-managing agencies

        ii)   coordinative--between governmental units and/or levels,

        iii)   enforcement--of federal laws and regulations

        iv)   operations--program administration, usually on non-federal lands,

        v)   planning--creating, reviewing or promoting,

        vi)   policy/promotional--usually advisory

vii)   regulatory--usually of utilities, transportation, and private industry,

viii)   research--both "in-house" and by grant programs to research institutions,

ix)   service--usually directly to the individuals needing assistance, but also to industry and local governments, and

x)   study groups--usually ad hoc committees or commissions created by Congress or the President to investigate a particular problem.

2.12b   Twenty-five agencies from 2.11a and b are selected here on the basis of major responsibilities in resources management activities, and are analyzed in Table 5.

2.12c   Very few of these are single-functioned, such as the Office of Water Resources Research and study groups which, although they may have a profound effect on the future activities of the Federal government, are usually short-lived and not sufficiently stereotyped for a generalized discussion here.

2.12d   Most of the agencies have multiple functions, which may conflict with one another. Thus,

i)   between Executive Departments, such as the Department of Agriculture in which a unit is charged with operating the Soil Bank program to pay farmers to take land out of production while the Department of Interior is assisting in bringing more land into production through irrigation;

ii)   the Federal Power Commission is charged both with promoting federal power development and regulating private; and

FUNCTIONS OF SELECTED FEDERAL AGENCIES

Agency	admini-strative (lands)	coordi-native	enforce-ment	opera-tional	plan-ning	policy/promo-tional	regu-latory	research	service	study group
AEC						X	X	X		
ARS							X	X		
BIA	X									
BIM	X									
BR				X					X	
CG			X							
CE			X	X					X	
CEQ		X	X			X	X	X	X	
EPA		X	X			X	X	X	X	
FEWS								X	X	
FDA	X		X				X	X		
FS	X	X	X			X	X	X	X	
FIARBC								X		X
FPC	X					X	X			
NPS	X									
NWC									X	X
NES		X						X	X	
OEP		X		X		X		X	X	
OSW		X				X		X	X	
OWRR								X	X	
PHS						X	X	X	X	
PLLRC										X
SCS				X	X			X	X	X
TVA	X			X	X		X		X	
WRC		X			X					

Atomic Energy Commission; Agricultural Research Service; Bureau of Indian Affairs; Bureau of Land Management; Bureau of Reclamation; Coast Guard; Corps of Engineers; Council on Environmental Quality; Environmental Protection Agency; Fish and Wildlife Service; Food and Drug Administration; Forest Service; Federal Inter-Agency River Basin Commission (now defunct); Federal Power Commission; National Park Service; National Weather Commission; National Weather Service; Office of Emergency Preparedness (see Planning); Office of Saline Water; Office of Water Resources Research; Public Health Service; Public Land Law Review Commission (defunct); Soil Conservation Service; Tennessee Valley Authority, and the Water Resources Council).

FEB, 1970; rev. 1/73

61

iii) the Corps of Engineers is charged with the responsibilities of flood control which requires dam-building and navigation which requires regulating channel obstructions.

2.12e Conflict of interest within agencies (and coincidental interests on the part of regulatory agencies and the private concerns they regulate) prompted the courts' interpretation that impact statements must be prepared by the action-taking agency (*Greene County Planning Board v. FPC*) so that the statement will not be "self-serving" (Anderson, 1973).

2.13 Activities of the Federal Agencies include a wide variety of responsibilities which involve several types of actions, including:

2.13a physical construction, as in the case of dams, military installations, navigation conveniences, etc.;

2.13b intentional modification of the environment in the process of resource management, such as stream-dredging, forest cutting, prescribed burning, or wetlands drainage;

2.13c providing funds for private industry or some other governmental unit to accomplish either of the above;

2.13d exercising indirect control over resource development by

i) granting (or cancelling) permits or licenses for power plants, rights-of-way, oil leases, etc.;

ii) imposing zoning regulations, including establishing or changing Federal land boundaries, or plans therefore, and

iii) setting standards.

2.13e   It is important to recognize that
while specific actions (2.13a) may
have a monumental environmental impact,
that impact is usually localized in
contrast to the seemingly innoccuous
promulgation of standards which may,
in fact, have far greater ramifications
and which are also classed as major
actions.

2.14   Interpretation and application of the provisions
of NEPA by the courts may be viewed as referring
to this rough classification (2.13) of actions.

2.14a   Thus, a 102 statement is required for

a)   all types of physical construction
by Federal agencies;

b)   all types of intentional environmental modification by the Federal
administrative agencies;

c)   providing funds or permits for
either of the above;

d)   granting of permits or licenses, and

e)   for plans or zoning regulations, or
review thereof, by the Federal agency.

2.14b   The exception to adherence to NEPA is
generalized from the decision in *Cohen v.
Price Commission* (337 F.2d 1242, 1972)
in that temporary agencies and/or
emergency decisions are exempted along
with matters pertaining to National Security.

2.15   The interaction of the existing Federal structure,
NEPA, and the changing role of public participation in governmental activities affecting resources management is likely to require some substantial procedural changes.

2.15a   Certain agencies that have ignored
public opinion to a greater or lesser
extent, in the past, are going to have
to make a concerted effort to assure
the public that they are playing and
can play a useful role. This is par-

ticularly true of

i)   the Bureau of Reclamation, whioh
has done almost all of its public
relations contact work with the
public through units of local
government, usually irrigation
districts, with which it conducts
most of its business, and

ii)   the regulatory agencies, including
the Atomic Energy Commission and
the Federal Power Commission especially, which are now responsible
for preparation of 102 statements
themselves and generally subject
to greater public scrutiny.

2.15b   The administrative agencies, notably the
Forest Service, Soil Conservation Service,
and National Park Service, which have
prided themselves on having a tradition
of "being in tune with public opinion"
have to undergo a major change of attitude according to the "Bolle Report"
(Craig, 1971). The Forest Service, in
particular, has a tradition of considering itself a model bureauocracy composed
largely of competent professionals who
have worked their way up through the
ranks (Kaufman, 1960). This agency has
neglected to allow the public more than
perfunctory input into plans and operations on the National Forests, and consequently has undergone considerable
attack in the past decade. Specific
procedures long accepted by these agencies
such as prescribed burning, clear-cutting,
channel straightening, small dam construction, clearing for vistas, zoning
for recreational uses of different types,
and transportation facilities extensions
and improvements are currently coming
under public scrutiny and NEPA has been
testily invoked (Anderson, 1973).

2.15c   The Corps of Engineers, singled out here
because of its long involvement in a
variety of resource management activities,
has made significant advances in culti-

vating public attitudes and in complying with NEPA in fact and in spirit. Part of this is because the Corps has a number of responsibilities (2.12) which keep its name before the public, and part is due to the fact that it still retains a well-used track around the Office of Management and Budget to the Congress for funds to back its programs (Laycock, 1970; Green, *et al*, 1970).

2.15d   For all agencies, established procedures, particularly hearings, will have to be carefully evaluated so as to better involve the public before threshhold determination (of whether or not a 102 statement must be filed) commences.

2.16   NEPA is expected to have a substantial effect on Federal agencies. Summarizing an informative and timely article by Smith (1971) "most resource management agencies realize that they are in deep trouble, ...essentially political. ....Since few bureauocracies readily accept a reduction of their budget or a drastic reorganization of their programs, it is not surprising that existing agencies are looking for ways to ensure their survival, and perhaps to improve their position by putting essentially unchanged programs in a new linguistic wrapping." Smith points out that NEPA has played a major role in bringing this situation about and questions whether simple lip service and minor adjustments will suffice. He gives some indications that "the politics of the environment" are really different from "the politics of resource management" and adds that if they "are fundamentally different in kind, ... then a theory of environmental administration will be required that both reinterprets present experience and provides the basis for some drastic, long-run alterations in administrative practices."

Opportunities for Governments

2.2   The National Environmental Policy Act has provided the Federal Government with the opportunity of greater efficiency, economy, and coordination of operation as well as a vehicle, indeed, a charge, to communicate more effectively with the publics that are served:

> · NEPA is a self-executing, full-disclosure law which is analagous to the law governing security exchange transactions; it is intended to improve the planning process, expand public participation in governmental decisions and sensitize the decision-makers to environmental consideration (Curlin and Hughes, 1973).

2.21   The efficiency of overall operation will unquestionably be improved, assuming NEPA is adhered to, owing to better decisions. This is due specifically to the requirements of Section 102(2)C which require examination of all reasonable alternatives along with minimization of adverse environmental impacts and avoidance of irretrievable and irreversible commitments of resources.

2.22   Greater economy may be achieved through this improved efficiency in operation and decison-making because of the opportunity of utilizing a tiered approach to the preparation of environmental impact statements for policies, programs, projects, and practices. This should ultimately remove the chaff from the environmental impact statement, making it a readable and useful document which represents the environment, complies with NEPA, and is simultaneously geared to the adjacent level vertically and keyed to parallel policies and implied implementation horizontally.

2.23   The opportunity of improved coordination within the Executive Branch agencies is that which has been sought through the succession of Coordination Acts referred to earlier and conceivably could lead to the eventual implementation of the recommendations of the Hoover Commission to combine the resource-managing agencies under on roof. Such could not be accomplished without full public trust, and NEPA may indeed provide that essential first step in this streamlining process.

2.24   The opportunity for better communications with the publics that are served by the Federal agencies is encouraged and required by NEPA and the agencies are charged, therefore, with keeping the publics informed; this is essential so that people will not feel "put upon" or "snowed" by the seemingly all-powerful agency.

2.3   The publics must provide the appropriate reaction
        to the agencies and respond thereto in a responsible
        manner.

    2.31   It is essential that the publics keep informed
            politically so as to understand the pressures
            placed upon the decision-makers in the agencies
            and the legislature; ecologically to appreciate
            our natural environment and heritage, and
            technologically to take advantage of new develop-
            ments and comprehensions of our way of life.

    2.32   The publics are responsible, too, to respond to
            agency activities by

        2.32a   understanding legislative charges in-
                cluding the sequence of current and
                developing policy-program-project
                practices schemes and to insure the
                diversity at all levels necessary to
                the maintenance of stability in the
                environment;

        2.32b   participating in decision-making in a
                responsible manner by assisting re-
                sponsible bureaucrats through letting
                them know interests, wants, and views;
                and by not abusing NEPA, for that Act
                was not intended to stop backyard in-
                roads on personal freedoms, and

        2.32c   adopting the recognition of conservation
                for what it is: a balance of natural
                resource exploitive and preserving
                policies, programs, projects, and prac-
                tices so as to match use over time with
                supply over time so that we and future
                generations may, indeed, live "in
                productive harmony."

LIST OF CASES

REFERENCES

Anderson, F. R. 1973. NEPA In the Courts. Johns Hopkins Press.
324 pp.

Anonymous, 1972. The Economic Impact of Pollution Control Report
prepared for the Council on Environmental Quality, Department
of Commerce, and E.P.A., U.S. Government Printing Office,
Washington, D.C. 332 pp.

Babcock, R. F., 1966. The Zoning Game. The University of
Wisconsin Press, Madison, Wisconsin. 202 pp.

Bates, M., 1960. The Forest and the Sea. Mentor Books, N.Y.
.216 pp.

Black, P. E., 1970. The Watershed in Principle. *Water Resources
Bulletin* 6(2): 465-77.

Brown, H., 1954. The Challenge of Man's Future. The Viking
Press, New York. 290 pp.

Clawson, M., 1963. Land and Water Recreation. Rand McNally
and Co., Chicago, Il. 144 pp.

Coyle, D. C., 1957. Conservation. Rutgers University Press,
New Brunswick, New Jersey. 284 pp.

Council on Environmental Quality, 1971.
Second Annual Report, Government Printing Office, Washington,
D.C. 360 pp.

Third Annual Report. ------------ 450 pp.

Fourth Annual Report. ----------- 499 pp.

Craig, J. B., 1971. Montana's Select Committee. *American Forests*
77(2):35ff.

Curlin, J. W. & Hughes, H. S., 1973. National Environmental
Policy Act of 1969: an analysis of proposed legislative
modifications, first session, 93d Congress. Environmental
Policy Division, Congressional Research Service, Library of
Congress, U. S. G. P. O., Washington, D. C. 78 pp.

Dasmann, R. F. 1962. Environmental Conservation. John Wiley &
Sons, Inc., New York. 307 pp.

DeLong, R. L., Gilmartin, W. G., and Simpson, J. G. 1973.
  Premature Births in California Sea Lions: Association with
  High Organochlorine Pollutant Residue Levels. *Science* 181:
  1168-70.

Eckstein, D.   1958. *Water Resources Development*. Harvard
  University Press, Cambridge, MA. 300 pp.

Environmental Defense Fund, 1973.   Progress Report Gilham
  Dam. *EDF Letter* July, 1973. p. 4.

Esposito, J. C., 1970.   Vanishing Air, Grossman Publishers,
  N.Y. 320 pp.

Garvey, G. 1972. *Energy, Ecology, Economy*. W. W. Norton
  & Co., Inc., N.Y. 235 pp.

Gustafson, A. F., *et al*, 1949. *Conservation In the United States*.
  Comstock Publishing Co., Ithaca, N.Y. 534 pp.

Haveman, R. H. 1965. *Water Resource Investment and the Public
  Interest*. Vanderbilt University Press, Nashville, TN. 199 pp.

Hawley, A. H. 1973. Ecology and Population, *Science* 179:1196.

Howe, C. W. 1971. Benefit-Cost Analysis for Water System
  Planning. Water Resources Monograph #2, American Geophysical
  Union, Washington, DC. 144 pp.

Green, M. J., Fallows, J. M., and Zwick, D. R., 1972. *Who Runs
  Congress?* Bantam Books, N.Y. 307 pp.

Jowett, D. 1972. *The Quantitative Assessment of Environmental
  Impacts*. Environmental Impact Analysis ed. by R. B. Ditton &
  T. I. Goodale, University of Wisconsin, Green Bay, pp. 127-136.

Kaufman, H. 1960. *The Forest Ranger*. The Johns Hopkins Press,
  Baltimore, MD. 259 pp.

Laycock, G. 1970. *The Diligent Destroyers*. Ballantine Books,
  Inc., NY. 243 pp.

Lichtenstein, E. P., Liang, T. T., and Anderegg, B. N., 1973.
  Synergism of insecticides by herbicides. *Science* 181:847-9.

Lindeman, R. L., 1942. The Trophic-Dynamic Aspect of Ecology.
  Ecology. 23:399-418.

Leopold, L. B. *et al*, 1971. A Procedure for Evaluating Environmental Impact. Geological Survey Circular 645, U. S. Dept. of the Interior, Washington, DC. 13 pp.

Lyons, B. 1955. Tomorrow's Birthright. Funk and Wagnalls Co., New York. 424 pp.

Marsh, G. P. 1874. The Earth As Modified by Human Action. Charles Scribner's Sons, New York. 629 pp.

Marshall, R. 1930. The Social Management of American Forests. League for Industrial Democracy, New York. 36 pp.

Office of the Federal Register, 1971. (rev. annually). U. S. Government Organizational Manual, National Archives & Records Service, General Services Administration, Washington, DC. 809 pp.

Osborn, F. 1949. Our Plundered Planet. Little Brown, and Co., Boston, MA. 217pp.

Pinchot, G. 1947. Breaking New Ground. Harcourt, Brace, and Co., New York. 522 pp.

Porter, E. 1969. Down the Colorado. E. P. Dutton & Co., Inc., New York. 168 pp.

Reitze, A. W. 1972. Environmental Law I. North American International, Washington, DC. 542 pp.

President's Water Resources Council, 1962. Policies, standards, and procedures in the formulation, evaluation, and review of plans of use and development of water and related land resources, S. D. No. 97 - 87th Congress, 2nd Session.

Resources for the Future, 1973. Three years of NEPA. *Resources*, No. 43, pp. 1-2.

Schad, T. M. 1968. Congressional Handling of Water Resources. *Congressional Record* H1276-84, February 21, 1968.

Schultz, A. M. **1967**. The Ecosystem as a Conceptual Tool in the Management of Natural Resources. In NATURAL RESOURCES: Quality and Quantity. Papers presented before a Faculty Seminar at the University of California, Berkely, CA. pp. 139-161.

Sorenson, J. C. 1971. A Framework for Identification and Control of Resource Degradation and Conflict in the Multiple Use of the Coastal Zone. Masters Thesis, University of California, Berkely, CA.

Sorenson, J. C. 1972. Some Procedures and Programs of Environmental Impact. In ENVIRONMENTAL IMPACT ANALYSIS: Philosophy and Methods, ed. by R. B. Ditton, and T. I. Goodale, University of Wisconsin, Madison. pp. 97-106.

Strahler, A. N., and Strahler, A. H., 1973. Environmental geoscience: Interaction Between Natural Systems and Man. Hamilton Publishing Co., Santa Barbara, CA. 511 pp.

Subcommittee on Benefits and Costs, 1950. Proposed Practices for Economic Analysis of River Basin Projects. Federal Inter-Agency River Basin Committee, Washington, DC. 85 pp.

Subcommittee on Fisheries and Wildlife Conservation. 1972. Administration of the National Environmental Policy Act, Appendix to Hearings, February 17, 25; May 24, Serial No. 92-25, USGPO, Washington, DC. 1887 pp.

Swift, H. H. 1962. From the Eagle's Wing. William Morrow and Co., N.Y. 287 pp.

U. S. Department of Agriculture, 1952. Highlights in the History of Forest Conservation. Forest Service, Agriculture Information Bulletin No. 83, Washington, DC. 23 pp.

Vogt, W. 1948. The Road to Survival. William Sloane & Associates, NY.

Water Resources Council, 1972. Summary Analysis of Public Response to the Proposed Principles and Standards.... 2120 L Street, N. W., Washington, DC. 135 pp.

Water Resources Council, 1973. Water and Related Land Resources: Establishment of Principles and Standards for Planning. *Federal Register* 38(174):24778-24869.

Westman, W. E., and Gifford, R. M., 1973. Environmental Impact: controlling the overall level. *Science* 181:819-25.

White, G. F. 1972. Environmental Impact Statements. *The Professional Geographer* XXLV (4): 306.

Wurster, C. F., & Wingate, D. B., 1968. DDT Residues and Declining Reproduction in the Bermuda Petrel. *Science* 159:979-981.

APPENDICES

APPENDIX A

The National Environmental Policy Act of 1969, Public Law 91-190 January 1, 1970 (42 U.S.C. 4321-4347)

An Act to establish a national policy for the environment, to provide for the establishment of a Council on Environmental Quality, and for other purposes.

Be it enacted by the Senate and House of Representatives of the United States of America in Congress assembled, That this Act may be cited as the "National Environmental Policy Act of 1969."

Purpose

Sec. 2. The purposes of this Act are: To declare a national policy which will encourage productive and enjoyable harmony between man and his environment; to promote efforts which will prevent or eliminate damage to the environment and biosphere and stimulate the health and welfare of man; to enrich the understanding of the ecological systems and natural resources important to the Nation; and to establish a Council on Environmental Quality.

Title i

Declaration of National Environmental Policy

Sec. 101. (a) The Congress, recognizing the profound impact of man's activity on the interrelations of all components of the natural environment, particularly the profound influences of population growth, high-density urbanization, industrial expansion, resource exploitation, and new and expanding technological advances and recognizing further the critical importance of restoring and maintaining environmental quality to the overall welfare and development of man, declares that it is the continuing policy of the Federal Government, in cooperation with State and local governments, and other concerned public and private organizations, to use all practicable means and measures, including financial and technical assistance, in a manner calculated to foster and promote the general welfare, to create and maintain conditions under which man and nature can exist in productive harmony, and fulfill the social, economic, and other requirements of present and future generations of Americans.

(b) In order to carry out the policy set forth in this Act, it is the continuing responsibility of the Federal Government to use all practicable means, consistent with other essential considerations of national policy, to improve and coordinate Federal plans, functions, programs, and resources to the end that the Nation may—

(1) Fulfill the responsibilities of each generation as trustee of the environment for succeeding generations;

(2) Assure for all Americans safe, healthful, productive, and esthetically and culturally pleasuring suroundings;

(3) Attain the widest range of beneficial uses of the environment without degradation, risk to health or safety, or other undesirable and unintended consequences;

(4) Preserve important historic, cultural, and natural aspects of our national heritage, and maintain, wherever possible, an environment which supports diversity, and variety of individual choice;

(5) Achieve a balance between population and resource use which will permit high standards of living and a wide sharing of life's amenities; and

(6) Enhance the quality of renewable resources and approach the maximum attainable recycling of depletable resources.

(c) The Congress recognizes that each person should enjoy a healthful environment and that each person has a responsibility to contribute to the preservation and enhancement of the environment.

Sec. 102. The Congress authorizes and directs that, to the fullest extent possible: (1) the policies, regulations, and public laws of the United States shall be interpreted and administered in accordance with the policies set forth in this Act, and (2) all agencies of the Federal Government shall—

(A) Utilize a systematic, interdisciplinary approach which will insure the integrated use of the natural and social sciences and the environmental design arts in planning and in decisionmaking which may have an impact on man's environment;

(B) Identify and develop methods and procedures, in consultation with the Council on Environmental Quality established by title II of this Act, which will insure that presently unquantified environmental amenities and values may be given appropriate consideration in decisionmaking along with economic and technical considerations;

(C) Include in every recommendation or report on proposals for legislation and other major Federal actions significantly affecting the quality of the human environment, a detailed statement by the responsible official on—

(i) The environmental impact of the proposed action,

(ii) Any adverse environmental effects which cannot be avoided should the proposal be implemented,

(iii) Alternatives to the proposed action,

(iv) The relationship between local short-term uses of man's environment and the maintenance and enhancement of long-term productivity, and

(v) Any irreversible and irretrievable commitments of resources which would be involved in the proposed action should it be implemented.

Prior to making any detailed statement, the responsible Federal official shall consult with and obtain the comments of any Federal agency which has jurisdiction by law or special expertise with respect to any environmental impact involved. Copies of such statement and the comments and views of the appropriate Federal, State, and local agencies, which are authorized to develop and enforce environmental standards, shall be made available to the President, the Council on Environmental Quality and to the public as provided by section 552 of title 5, United States Code, and shall accompany the proposal through the existing agency review processes;

(D) Study, develop, and describe appropriate alternatives to recommended courses of action in any proposal which involves unresolved conflicts concerning alternative uses of available resources;

(E) Recognize the worldwide and long-range character of environmental problems and, where consistent with the foreign policy of the United States, lend appropriate support to initiatives, resolutions, and programs designed to maximize international cooperation in anticipating and preventing a decline in the quality of mankind's world environment;

(F) Make available to States, counties, municipalities, institutions, and individuals, advice and information useful in restoring, maintaining, and enhancing the quality of the environment;

(G) Initiate and utilize ecological information in the planning and development of resource-oriented projects; and

(H) Assist the Council on Environmental Quality established by title II of this Act.

Sec. 103. All agencies of the Federal Government shall review their present statutory authority, administrative regulations, and current policies and procedures for the purpose of determining whether there are any deficiencies or inconsistencies therein which prohibit full compliance with the purposes and provisions of this Act and shall propose to the President not later than July 1, 1971, such measurers as may be necessary to bring thier authority and policies into conformity with the intent, purposes, and procedures set forth in this Act.

Sec. 104. Nothing in section 102 or 103 shall in any way affect the specific statutory obligations of any Federal agency (1) to comply with criteria or standards of environmental quality, (2) to coordinate or consult with any other Federal or State agency, or (3) to act, or refrain from acting contingent upon the recommendations or certification of any other Federal or State agency.

Sec. 105. The policies and goals set forth in this Act are supplementary to those set forth in existing authorizations of Federal agencies.

Title ii

Council on Environmental Quality

Sec. 201. The President shall transmit to the Congress annually beginning July 1, 1970, an Environmental Quality Report (hereinafter referred to as the "report") which shall set forth (1) the status and condition of the major natural, manmade, or altered environmental classes of the Nation, including, but not limited to, the air, the aquatic, including marine, estuarine, and fresh water, and the terrestrial environment, including, but not limited to, the forest, dryland, wetland, range, urban, suburban and rural environment; (2) current and foreseeable trends in the quality, management and utilization of such environments and the effects of those trends on the social, economic, and other requirements of the Nation; (3) the adequacy of available natural resources for fulfilling human and economic requirements of the Nation in the light of expected population pressures; (4) a review of the programs and activities (including regulatory activities) of the Federal Government, the State and local governments, and nongovernmental entities or individuals with particular reference to their effect on the environment and on the conservation, development and utilization of natural resources; and (5) a program for remedying the deficiencies of existing programs and activities, together with recommendations for legislation.

Sec. 202. There is created in the Executive Office of the President a Council on Environmental Quality (hereinafter referred to as the "Council"). The Council shall be composed of three members who shall be appointed by the President to serve at his pleasure, by and with the advice and consent of the Senate. The President shall designate one of the members of the Council to serve as Chairman. Each member shall be a person who, as a result of his training, experience, and attainments, is exceptionally well qualified to analyze and interpret environmental trends and information of all kinds; to appraise programs and activities of the Federal Government in the light of the policy set forth in title I of this Act; to be conscious of and responsive to the scientific, economic, social, esthetic, and cultural needs and interests of the Nation; and to formulate and recommend national policies to promote the improvement of the quality of the environment.

Sec. 203. The Council may employ such officers and employees as may be necessary to carry out its functions under this Act. In addition, the Council may employ and fix the compensation of such experts and consultants as may be necessary for the carrying out of its functions under this Act, in accordance with section 3109 of title 5, United States Code (but without regard to the last sentence thereof).

Sec. 204. It shall be the duty and function of the Council—

(1) To assist and advise the President in the preparation of the Environmental Quality Report required by section 201;

(2) To gather timely and authoritative information concerning the conditions and trends in the quality of the environment both current and prospective, to analyze and interpret such information for the purpose of determining whether such conditions and trends are interfering, or are likely to interfere, with the achievement of the policy set forth in title I of this Act, and to compile and submit to the President studies relating to such conditions and trends;

(3) To review and appraise the various programs and activities of the Federal Government in the light of the policy set forth in title I of this Act for the purpose of determining the extent to which such programs and activities are contributing to the achievement of such policy, and to make recommendations to the President with respect thereto;

(4) To develop and recommend to the President national policies to foster and promote the improvement of environmental quality to meet the conservation, social, economic, health, and other requirements and goals of the Nation;

(5) To conduct investigations, studies, surveys, research, and analyses relating to ecological systems and environmental quality;

(6) To document and define changes in the natural environment, including the plant and animal systems, and to accumulate necessary data and other information for a continuing analysis of these changes or trends and an interpretation of their underlying causes;

(7) To report at least once each year to the President on the state and condition of the environment; and

(8) To make and furnish such studies, reports thereon, and recommendations with respect to matters of policy and legislation as the President may request.

Sec. 205. In exercising its powers, functions, and duties under this Act, the Council shall—

(1) Consult with the Citizens' Advisory Committee on Environmental Quality established by Executive Order No. 11472, dated May 29, 1969, and with such representatives of science, industry, agriculture, labor, conservation organizations, State and local governments and other groups, as it deems advisable; and

(2) Utilize, to the fullest extent possible, the services, facilities and information (including statistical information) of public and private agencies and organizations, and individuals, in order that duplication of effort and expense may be avoided, thus assuring that the Council's activities will not unnecessarily overlap or conflict with similar activities authorized by law and performed by established agencies.

SEC. 206. Members of the Council shall serve full time and the Chairman of the Council shall be compensated at the rate provided for Level II of the Executive Schedule Pay Rates (5 U.S.C. 5313). The other members of the Council shall be compensated at the rate provided for Level IV of the Executive Schedule Pay Rates (5 U.S.C. 5315).

SEC. 207. There are authorized to be appropriated to carry out the provisions of this Act not to exceed $300,000 for fiscal year 1970, $700,000 for fiscal year 1971, and $1 million for each fiscal year thereafter.

Approved January 1, 1970.

Preparation of Environmental Impact Statements: Guidelines*

On May 2, 1973, the Council on Environmental Quality published in the FEDERAL REGISTER, for public comment, a proposed revision of its guidelines for the preparation of environmental impact statements. Pursuant to the National Environmental Policy Act (P.L. 91-190, 42 U.S.C. 4321 et seq.) and Executive Order 11514 (35 FR 4247) all Federal departments, agencies, and establishments are required to prepare such statements in connection with their proposals for legislation and other major Federal actions significantly affecting the quality of the human environment. The authority for the Council's guidelines is set forth below in § 1500.1. The specific policies to be implemented by the guidelines is set forth below in § 1500.2.

The Council received numerous comments on its proposed guidelines from environmental groups, Federal, State, and local agencies, industry, and private individuals. Two general themes were presented in the majority of the comments. First, the Council should increase the opportunity for public involvement in the impact statement process. Second, the Council should provide more detailed guidance on the responsibilities of Federal agencies in light of recent court decisions interpreting the Act. The proposed guidelines have been revised in light of the specific comments relating to these general themes, as well as other comments received, and are now being issued in final form.

The guidelines will appear in the Code of Federal Regulations in Title 40, Chapter V, at Part 1500. They are being codified, in part, because they affect State and local governmental agencies, environmental groups, industry, and private individuals, in addition to Federal agencies, to which they are specifically directed, and the resultant need to make them widely and readily available.

Sec.

*38 Fed. Reg. 20550–20562, August 1, 1973.

AUTHORITY: National Environmental Act (P.L. 91–190, 42 U.S.C. 4321 et seq.) and Executive Order 11514.

§ 1500.1 Purpose and authority.

(a) This directive provides guidelines to Federal departments, agencies, and establishments for preparing detailed environmental statements on proposals for legislation and other major Federal actions significantly affecting the quality of the human environment as required by section 102(2)(C) of the National Environmental Policy Act (P.L. 91–190, 42 U.S.C. 4321 et. seq.) (hereafter "the Act"). Underlying the preparation of such environmental statements is the mandate of both the Act and Executive Order 11514 (35 FR 4247) of March 5, 1970, that all Federal agencies, to the fullest extent possible, direct their policies, plans and programs to protect and enhance environmental quality. Agencies are required to view their actions in a manner calculated to encourage productive and enjoyable harmony between man and his environment, to promote efforts preventing or eliminating damage to the environment and biosphere and stimulating the health and welfare of man, and to enrich the understanding of the ecological systems and natural resources important to the Nation. The objective of section 102(2)(C) of the Act and of these guidelines is to assist agencies in implementing these policies. This requires agencies to build into their decisionmaking process, beginning at the earliest possible point, an appropriate and careful consideration of the environmental aspects of proposed action in order that adverse environmental effects may be avoided or minimized and environmental quality previously lost may be restored. This directive also provides guidance to Federal, State, and local agencies and the public in commenting on statements prepared under these guidelines.

(b) Pursuant to section 204(3) of the Act the Council on Environmental Quality (hereafter "the Council") is assigned the duty and function of reviewing and appraising the programs and activities of the Federal Government, in the light of the Act's policy, for the purpose of determining the extent to which such programs and activities are contributing to the achievement of such policy, and to make recommendations to the President with respect thereto. Section 102(2)(B) of the Act directs all Federal agencies to identify and develop methods and procedures, in consultation with the Council, to insure that unquantified environmental values be given appropriate consideration in decisionmaking along with economic and technical considerations; section 102(2)(C) of the Act directs that copies of all environmental impact statements be filed with the Council; and section 102(2)(H) directs all Federal agencies to assist the Council in the performance of its functions. These provisions have been supplemented in sections 3(h) and (i) of Executive Order 11514 by directions that the Council issue guidelines to Federal agencies for preparation of environmental impact statements and such other instructions to agencies and requests for reports and information as may be required to carry out the Council's responsibilities under the Act.

§ 1500.2 Policy.

(a) As early as possible and in all cases prior to agency decision concerning recommendations or favorable reports on proposals for (1) legislation significantly affecting the quality of the human environment (see §§ 1500.5(i) and 1500.12) (hereafter "legislative actions") and (2) all other major Federal actions significantly affecting the quality of the human environment (hereafter "administrative actions"), Federal agencies will, in consultation with other appropriate Federal, State and local agencies and the public assess in detail the potential environmental impact.

(b) Initial assessments of the environmental impacts of proposed action should be undertaken concurrently with initial technical and economic studies and, where required, a draft environmental impact statement prepared and circulated for comment in time to accompany the proposal through the existing agency review processes for such action. In this process, Federal agencies shall:

(1) Provide for circulation of draft environmental statements to other Federal, State, and local agencies and for their availability to the public in accordance with the provisions of these guidelines; (2) consider the comments of the agencies and the public; and (3) issue final environmental impact statements responsive to the comments received. The purpose of this assessment and consultation process is to provide agencies and other decisionmakers as well as members of the public with an understanding of the potential environmental effects of proposed actions, to avoid or minimize adverse effects wherever possible, and to restore or enhance environmental quality to the fullest extent practicable. In particular, agencies should use the environmental impact statement process to explore alternative actions that will avoid or minimize adverse impacts and to evaluate both the long- and short-range implications of proposed actions to man, his physical and social surroundings, and to nature. Agencies should consider the results of their environmental assessments along with their assessments of the net economic, technical and other benefits of proposed actions and use all practicable means, consistent with other essential considerations of national policy, to restore environmental quality as well as to avoid or minimize undesirable consequences for the environment.

§ 1500.3 Agency and OMB procedures.

(a) Pursuant to section 2(f) of Executive Order 11514, the heads of Federal agencies have been directed to proceed with measures required by section 102 (2) (C) of the Act. Previous guidelines of the Council directed each agency to establish its own formal procedures for (1) identifying those agency actions requiring environmental statements, the appropriate time prior to decision for the consultations required by section 102 (2) (C) and the agency review process for which environmental statements are to be available, (2) obtaining information required in their preparation, (3) designating the officials who are to be responsible for the statements, (4) consulting with and taking account of the comments of appropriate Federal, State and local agencies and the public, including obtaining the comment of the Administrator of the Environmental Protection Agency when required under section 309 of the Clean Air Act, as amended, and (5) meeting the requirements of section 2(b) of Executive Order

11514 for providing timely public information on Federal plans and programs with environmental impact. Each agency, including both departmental and subdepartmental components having such procedures, shall review its procedures and shall revise them, in consultation with the Council, as may be necessary in order to respond to requirements imposed by these revised guidelines as well as by such previous directives. After such consultation, proposed revisions of such agency procedures shall be published in the FEDERAL REGISTER no later than October 30, 1973. A minimum 45-day period for public comment shall be provided, followed by publication of final procedures no later than forty-five (45) days after the conclusion of the comment period. Each agency shall submit seven (7) copies of all such procedures to the Council. Any future revision of such agency procedures shall similarly be proposed and adopted only after prior consultation with the Council and, in the case of substantial revision, opportunity for public comment. All revisions shall be published in the FEDERAL REGISTER.

(b) Each Federal agency should consult, with the assistance of the Council and the Office of Management and Budget if desired, with other appropriate Federal agencies in the development and revision of the above procedures so as to achieve consistency in dealing with similar activities and to assure effective coordination among agencies in their review of proposed activities. Where applicable, State and local review of such agency procedures should be conducted pursuant to procedures established by Office of Management and Budget Circular No. A-85.

(c) Existing mechanisms for obtaining the views of Federal, State, and local agencies on proposed Federal actions should be utilized to the maximum extent practicable in dealing with environmental matters. The Office of Management and Budget will issue instructions, as necessary, to take full advantage of such existing mechanisms.

§ 1500.4 Federal agencies included; effect of the Act on existing agency mandates.

(a) Section 102(2) (C) of the Act applies to all agencies of the Federal Government. Section 102 of the Act provides that "to the fullest extent possible: (1) The policies, regulations, and public laws of the United States shall be interpreted and administered in accordance with the policies set forth in this Act," and section 105 of the Act provides that "the policies and goals set forth in this Act are supplementary to those set forth in existing authorizations of Federal agencies." This means that each agency shall interpret the provisions of the Act as a supplement to its existing authority and as a mandate to view traditional policies and missions in the light of the Act's national environmental objectives. In accordance with this purpose, agencies should continue to review their policies, procedures, and regulations and to revise them as necessary to ensure full compliance with the purposes and provisions of the Act. The phrase "to the fullest extent possible" in section 102 is meant to make clear that each agency of the Federal Government shall comply with that section unless existing law applicable to the agency's operations expressly prohibits or makes compliance impossible.

§ 1500.5 Types of actions covered by the Act.

(a) "Actions" include but are not limited to:

(1) Recommendations or favorable reports relating to legislation including requests for appropriations. The requirement for following the section 102 (2)(C) procedure as elaborated in these guidelines applies to both (i) agency recommendations on their own proposals for legislation (see § 1500.12); and (ii) agency reports on legislation initiated elsewhere. In the latter case only the agency which has primary responsibility for the subject matter involved will prepare an environmental statement.

(2) New and continuing projects and program activities: directly undertaken by Federal agencies; or supported in whole or in part through Federal contracts, grants, subsidies, loans, or other forms of funding assistance (except where such assistance is solely in the form of general revenue sharing funds, distributed under the State and Local Fiscal Assistance Act of 1972, 31 U.S.C. 1221 et. seq. with no Federal agency control over the subsequent use of such funds); or involving a Federal lease, permit, license certificate or other entitlement for use.

(3) The making, modification, or establishment of regulations, rules, procedures, and policy.

§ 1500.6 Identifying major actions significantly affecting the environment.

(a) The statutory clause "major Federal actions significantly affecting the quality of the human environment" is to be construed by agencies with a view to the overall, cumulative impact of the action proposed, related Federal actions and projects in the area, and further actions contemplated. Such actions may be localized in their impact, but if there is potential that the environment may be significantly affected, the statement is to be prepared. Proposed major actions, the enviornmental impact of which is likely to be highly controversial, should be covered in all cases. In considering what constitutes major action significantly affecting the environment, agencies should bear in mind that the effect of many Federal decisions about a project or complex of projects can be individually limited but cumulatively considerable. This can occur when one or more agencies over a period of years puts into a project individually minor but collectively major resources, when one decision involving a limited amount of money is a precedent for action in much larger cases or represents a decision in principle about a future major course of action, or when several Government agencies individually make decisions about partial aspects of a major action. In all such cases, an environmental statement should be prepared if it is reasonable to anticipate a cumulatively significant impact on the environment from Federal action. The Council, on the basis of a written assessment of the impacts involved, is available to assist agencies in determining whether specific actions require impact statements.

(b) Section 101(b) of the Act indicates the broad range of aspects of the environment to be surveyed in any assessment of significant effect. The Act also indicates that adverse significant effects include those that degrade the quality of the environment, curtail the range of beneficial uses of the environment, and serve short-term, to the disadvantage of long-term, environmental goals. Significant effects can also include actions which may have both beneficial and detrimental effects, even if on balance the agency believes that the effect will be beneficial. Significant effects also include secondary effects, as described more fully, for example, in § 1500.8(a) (iii)(B). The significance of a proposed action may also vary with the setting, with the result that an action that would have little impact in an urban setting may be significant in a rural setting or vice versa. While a precise definition of environmental "significance," valid in all contexts, is not possible, effects to be considered in assessing significance in-

ude, but are not limited to, those out-
ned in Appendix II of these guidelines.
(c) Each of the provisions of the Act,
:cept section 102(2)(C), applies to all
:deral agency actions. Section 102(2)
:) requires the preparation of a detailed
vironmental impact statement in the
se of "major Federal actions signifi-
ntly affecting the quality of the human
vironment." The identification of
ajor actions significantly affecting the
vironment is the responsibility of each
:deral agency, to be carried out against
e background of its own particular op-
·ations. The action must be a (1)
najor" action, (2) which is a "Federal
tion," (3) which has a "significant" ef-
ct, and (4) which involves the "quality
the human environment." The words
najor" and "significantly" are intended
imply thresholds of importance and
ıpact that must be met before a state-
.ent is required. The action causing the
ıpact must also be one where there
sufficient Federal control and respon-
bility to constitute "Federal action" in
ontrast to cases where such Federal
ontrol and responsibility are not present
s, for example, when Federal funds are
stributed in the form of general reve-
ue sharing to be used by State and local
overnments (see § 1500.5(ii)). Finally,
ne action must be one that significantly
Tects the quality of the human envi-
onment either by directly affecting
uman beings or by indirectly affecting
uman beings through adverse effects
n the environment. Each agency should
eview the typical classes of actions that
undertakes and, in consultation with
ıe Council, should develop specific cri-
eria and methods for identifying those
ctions likely to require environmental
:atements and those actions likely not
o require environmental statements.
ormally this will involve:

(i) Making an initial assessment of
ıe environmental impacts typically as-
ociated with principal types of agency
ction.

(ii) Identifying on the basis of this
ssessment, types of actions which nor-
aally do, and types of actions which nor-
aally do not, require statements.

(iii) With respect to remaining actions
hat may require statements depending
n the circumstances, and those actions
etermined under the preceding para-
raph (C)(4)(ii) of this section as likely
o require statements, identifying: (a)
hat basic information needs to be
athered; (b) how and when such in-
ormation is to be assembled and ana-
zed; and (c) on what bases environ-

mental assessments and decisions to prepare impact statements will be made.
Agencies may either include this substantive guidance in the procedures issued pursuant to § 1500.3(a) of these
guidelines, or issue such guidance as
supplemental instructions to aid relevant
agency personnel in implementing the
impact statement process. Pursuant to
§ 1500.14 of these guidelines, agencies
shall report to the Council by June 30,
1974, on the progress made in developing
such substantive guidance.

(d) (1) Agencies should give careful
attention to identifying and defining the
purpose and scope of the action which
would most appropriately serve as the
subject of the statement. In many cases,
broad program statements will be required in order to assess the environmental effects of a number of individual
actions on a given geographical area (e.g.,
coal leases), or environmental impacts
that are generic or common to a series
of agency actions, maintenance or
waste handling practices), or the overall impact of a large-scale program or
chain of contemplated projects (e.g.,
major lengths of highway as opposed to
small segments). Subsequent statements
on major individual actions will be necessary where such actions have significant environmental impacts not adequately evaluated in the program
statement.

(2) Agencies engaging in major technology research and development programs should develop procedures for
periodic evaluation to determine when a
program statement is required for such
programs. Factors to be considered in
making this determination include the
magnitude of Federal investment in the
program, the likelihood of widespread
application of the technology, the degree
of environmental impact which would
occur if the technology were widely applied, and the extent to which continued
investment in the new technology is
likely to restrict future alternatives.
Statements must be written late enough
in the development process to contain
meaningful information, but early
enough so that this information can
practically serve as an input in the decision-making process. Where it is anticipated that a statement may ultimately
be required but that its preparation is
still premature, the agency should prepare an evaluation briefly setting forth
the reasons for its determination that a
statement is not yet necessary. This evaluation should be periodically updated,
particularly when significant new information becomes available concerning the

potential environmental impact of the program. In any case, a statement must be prepared before research activities have reached a stage of investment or commitment to implementation likely to determine subsequent development or restrict later alternatives. Statements on technology research and development programs should include an analysis not only of alternative forms of the same technology that might reduce any adverse environmental impacts but also of alternative technologies that would serve the same function as the technology under consideration. Efforts should be made to involve other Federal agencies and interested groups with relevant expertise in the preparation of such statements because the impacts and alternatives to be considered are likely to be less well defined than in other types of statements.

(e) In accordance with the policy of the Act and Executive Order 11514 agencies have a responsibility to develop procedures to insure the fullest practicable provision of timely public information and understanding of Federal plans and programs with environmental impact in order to obtain the views of interested parties. In furtherance of this policy, agency procedures should include an appropriate early notice system for informing the public of the decision to prepare a draft environmental statement on proposed administrative actions (and for soliciting comments that may be helpful in preparing the statement) as soon as is practicable after the decision to prepare the statement is made. In this connection, agencies should: (1) maintain a list of administrative actions for which environmental statements are being prepared; (2) revise the list at regular intervals specified in the agency's procedures developed pursuant to § 1500.3(a) of these guidelines (but not less than quarterly) and transmit each such revision to the Council; and (3) make the list available for public inspection on request. The Council will periodically publish such lists in the FEDERAL REGISTER. If an agency decides that an environmental statement is not necessary for a proposed action (i) which the agency has identified pursuant to § 1500.6(c)(4)(ii) as normally requiring preparation of a statement, (ii) which is similar to actions for which the agency has prepared a significant number of statements, (iii) which the agency has previously announced would be the subject of a statement, or (iv) for which the agency has made a negative determination in response to a request from

the Council pursuant to § 1500.11(f), the agency shall prepare a publicly available record briefly setting forth the agency's decision and the reasons for that determination. Lists of such negative determinations, and any evaluations, made pursuant to § 1500.6 which conclude that preparation of a statement is not yet timely, shall be prepared and made available in the same manner as provided in this subsection for lists of statements under preparation.

§ 1500.7   Preparing draft environmental statements; public hearings.

(a) Each environmental impact statement shall be prepared and circulated in draft form for comment in accordance with the provisions of these guidelines. The draft statement must fulfill and satisfy to the fullest extent possible at the time the draft is prepared the requirements established for final statements by section 102(2)(C). (Where an agency has an established practice of declining to favor an alternative until public comments on a proposed action have been received, the draft environmental statement may indicate that two or more alternatives are under consideration.) Comments received shall be carefully evaluated and considered in the decision process. A final statement with substantive comments attached shall then be issued and circulated in accordance with applicable provisions of §§ 1500.10, 1500.11, or 1500.12. It is important that draft environmental statements be prepared and circulated for comment and furnished to the Council as early as possible in the agency review process in order to permit agency decisionmakers and outside reviewers to give meaningful consideration to the environmental issues involved. In particular, agencies should keep in mind that such statements are to serve as the means of assessing the environmental impact of proposed agency actions, rather than as a justification for decisions already made. This means that draft statements on administrative actions should be prepared and circulated for comment prior to the first significant point of decision in the agency review process. For major categories of agency action, this point should be identified in the procedures issued pursuant to § 1500.3(a). For major categories of projects involving an applicant and identified pursuant to § 1500.6 (c)(c)(ii) as normally requiring the preparation of a statement, agencies should include in their procedures provisions limiting actions which an applicant is permitted to take prior to completion

d review of the final statement with
spect to his application.

(b) Where more than one agency (1)
rectly sponsors an action, or is directly
volved in an action through funding,
censes, or permits, or (2) is involved in
group of actions directly related to each
her because of their functional inter-
ependence and geographical proximity,
onsideration should be given to prepar-
g one statement for all the Federal
ctions involved (see § 1500.6(d)(1)).
gencies in such cases should consider
e possibility of joint preparation of a
atement by all agencies concerned, or
esignation of a single "lead agency"
assume supervisory responsibility for
reparation of the statement. Where a
ad agency prepares the statement, the
her agencies involved should provide
ssistance with respect to their areas of
urisdiction and expertise. In either case,
e statement should contain an en-
ironmental assessment of the full range
Federal actions involved, should reflect
e views of all participating agencies,
nd should be prepared before major or
reversible actions have been taken by
ny of the participating agencies. Fac-
ors relevant in determining an appro-
riate lead agency include the time
equence in which the agencies become
volved, the magnitude of their respec-
ve involvement, and their relative ex-
ertise with respect to the project's en-
ironmental effects. As necessary, the
ouncil will assist in resolving questions
responsibility for statement prepara-
ion in the case of multi-agency actions.
ederal Regional Councils, agencies and
he public are encouraged to bring to the
ttention of the Council and other rele-
ant agencies appropriate situations
here a geographic or regionally focused
tatement would be desirable because of
he cumulative environmental effects
kely to result from multi-agency actions
n the area.

(c) Where an agency relies on an ap-
licant to submit initial environmental
nformation, the agency should assist the
pplicant by outlining the types of infor-
ation required. In all cases, the agency
hould make its own evaluation of the
nvironmental issues and take respon-
ibility for the scope and content of draft
nd final environmental statements.

(d) Agency procedures developed pur-
uant to § 1500.3(a) of these guidelines
hould indicate as explicitly as possible
those types of agency decisions or actions
which utilize hearings as part of the normal agency review process, either as a
result of statutory requirement or agency
practice. To the fullest extent possible,

all such hearings shall include consideration of the environmental aspects of the
proposed action. Agency procedures shall
also specifically include provision for
public hearings on major actions with
environmental impact, whenever appropriate, and for providing the public with
relevant information, including information on alternative courses of action. In
deciding whether a public hearing is appropriate, an agency should consider:
(1) The magnitude of the proposal in
terms of economic costs, the geographic
area involved, and the uniqueness or size
of commitment of the resources involved;
(2) the degree of interest in the proposal, as evidenced by requests from the
public and from Federal, State and local
authorities that a hearing be held; (3)
the complexity of the issue and the likelihood that information will be presented
at the hearing which will be of assistance to the agency in fulfilling its responsibilities under the Act; and (4) the
extent to which public involvement already has been achieved through other
means, such as earlier public hearings,
meetings with citizen representatives,
and/or written comments on the proposed action. Agencies should make any
draft environmental statements to be issued available to the public at least
fifteen (15) days prior to the time of such
hearings.

§ 1500.8 Content of environmental
statements.

(a) The following points are to be
covered:

(1) A description of the proposed action, a statement of its purposes, and a
description of the environment affected,
including information, summary technical data, and maps and diagrams where
relevant, adequate to permit an assessment of potential environmental impact
by commenting agencies and the public.
Highly technical and specialized analyses and data should be avoided in the
body of the draft impact statement. Such
materials should be attached as appendices or footnoted with adequate
bibliographic references. The statement
should also succinctly describe the environment of the area affected as it exists
prior to a proposed action, including
other Federal activities in the area affected by the proposed action which are
related to the proposed action. The interrelationships and cumulative environmental impacts of the proposed action
and other related Federal projects shall
be presented in the statement. The
amount of detail provided in such descriptions should be commensurate with
the extent and expected impact of the

action, and with the amount of information required at the particular level of decisionmaking (planning, feasibility, design, etc.). In order to ensure accurate descriptions and environmental assessments, site visits should be made where feasible. Agencies should also take care to identify, as appropriate, population and growth ch... cteristics of the affected area and any population and growth assumptions used to justify the project or program or to determine secondary population and growth impacts resulting from the proposed action and its alternatives (see paragraph (a)(1)(3)(ii), of this section). In discussing these population aspects, agencies should give consideration to using the rates of growth in the region of the project contained in the projection compiled for the Water Resources Council by the Bureau of Economic Analysis of the Department of Commerce and the Economic Research Service of the Department of Agriculture (the "OBERS" projection). In any event it is essential that the sources of data used to identify, quantify or evaluate any and all environmental consequences be expressly noted.

(2) The relationship of the proposed action to land use plans, policies, and controls for the affected area. This requires a discussion of how the proposed action may conform or conflict with the objectives and specific terms of approved or proposed Federal, State, and local land use plans, policies, and controls, if any, for the area affected including those developed in response to the Clean Air Act or the Federal Water Pollution Control Act Amendments of 1972. Where a conflict or inconsistency exists, the statement should describe the extent to which the agency has reconciled its proposed action with the plan, policy or control, and the reasons why the agency has decided to proceed notwithstanding the absence of full reconciliation.

(3) The probable impact of the proposed action on the environment.

(i) This requires agencies to assess the positive and negative effects of the proposed action as it affects both the national and international environment. The attention given to different environmental factors will vary according to the nature, scale, and location of proposed actions. Among factors to consider should be the potential effect of the action on such aspects of the environment as those listed in Appendix II of these guidelines. Primary attention should be given in the statement to discussing those factors most evidently impacted by the proposed action.

(ii) Secondary or indirect, as well as primary or direct, consequences for the environment should be included in the analysis. Many major Federal actions, in particular those that involve the construction or licensing of infrastructure investments (e.g., highways, airports, sewer systems, water resource projects, etc.), stimulate or induce secondary effects in the form of associated investments and changed patterns of social and economic activities. Such secondary effects, through their impacts on existing community facilities and activities, through inducing new facilities and activities, or through changes in natural conditions, may often be even more substantial than the primary effects of the original action itself. For example, the effects of the proposed action on population and growth may be among the more significant secondary effects. Such population and growth impacts should be estimated if expected to be significant (using data identified as indicated in § 1500.8(a)(1)) and an assessment made of the effect of any possible change in population patterns or growth upon the resource base, including land use, water, and public services, of the area in question.

(4) Alternatives to the proposed action, including, where relevant, those not within the existing authority of the responsible agency. (Section 102(2)(D) of the Act requires the responsible agency to "study, develop, and describe appropriate alternatives to recommended courses of action in any proposal which involves unresolved conflicts concerning alternative uses of available resources"). A rigorous exploration and objective evaluation of the environmental impacts of all reasonable alternative actions, particularly those that might enhance environmental quality or avoid some or all of the adverse environmental effects, is essential. Sufficient analysis of such alternatives and their environmental benefits, costs and risks should accompany the proposed action through the agency review process in order not to foreclose prematurely options which might enhance environmental quality or have less detrimental effects. Examples of such alternatives include: the alternative of taking no action or of postponing action pending further study; alternatives requiring actions of a significantly different nature which would provide similar benefits with different environmental impacts (e.g., nonstructural alternatives to flood control programs, or mass transit alternatives to highway construction); alternatives related to different designs

details of the proposed action which would present different environmental impacts (e.g., cooling ponds vs. cooling towers for a power plant or alternatives at will significantly conserve energy); alternative measures to provide for compensation of fish and wildlife losses, including the acquisition of land, waters, and interests therein. In each case, the analysis should be sufficiently detailed to reveal the agency's comparative evaluation of the environmental benefits, costs and risks of the proposed action and each reasonable alternative. Where an existing impact statement already contains such an analysis, its treatment of alternatives may be incorporated provided that such treatment is current and relevant to the precise purpose of the proposed action.

(5.) Any probable adverse environmental effects which cannot be avoided (such as water or air pollution, undesirable land use patterns, damage to life systems, urban congestion, threats to health or other consequences adverse to the environmental goals set out in section 101 (b) of the Act). This should be a brief section summarizing in one place those effects discussed in paragraph (a) (3) of this section that are adverse and unavoidable under the proposed action. Included for purposes of contrast should be a clear statement of how other avoidable adverse effects discussed in paragraph (a) (2) of this section will be mitigated.

(6) The relationship between local short-term uses of man's environment and the maintenance and enhancement of long-term productivity. This section should contain a brief discussion of the extent to which the proposed action involves tradeoffs between short-term environmental gains at the expense of long-term losses, or vice versa, and a discussion of the extent to which the proposed action forecloses future options. In this context short-term and long-term do not refer to any fixed time periods, but should be viewed in terms of the environmentally significant consequences of the proposed action.

(7) Any irreversible and irretrievable commitments of resources that would be involved in the proposed action should it be implemented. This requires the agency to identify from its survey of unavoidable impacts in paragraph (a) (5) of this section the extent to which the action irreversibly curtails the range of potential uses of the environment. Agencies should avoid construing the term "resources" to mean only the labor and materials devoted to an action. "Resources" also means the natural and cultural resources committed to loss or destruction by the action.

(8) An indication of what other interests and considerations of Federal policy are thought to offset the adverse environmental effects of the proposed action identified pursuant to paragraphs (a) (3) and (5) of this section. The statement should also indicate the extent to which these stated countervailing benefits could be realized by following reasonable alternatives to the proposed action (as identified in paragraph (a) (4) of this section) that would avoid some or all of the adverse environmental effects. In this connection, agencies that prepare cost-benefit analyses of proposed actions should attach such analyses, or summaries thereof, to the environmental impact statement, and should clearly indicate the extent to which environmental costs have not been reflected in such analyses.

(b) In developing the above points agencies should make every effort to convey the required information succinctly in a form easily understood, both by members of the public and by public decisionmakers, giving attention to the substance of the information conveyed rather than to the particular form, or length, or detail of the statement. Each of the above points, for example, need not always occupy a distinct section of the statement if it is otherwise adequately covered in discussing the impact of the proposed action and its alternatives—which items should normally be the focus of the statement. Draft statements should indicate at appropriate points in the text any underlying studies, reports, and other information obtained and considered by the agency in preparing the statement including any cost-benefit analyses prepared by the agency, and reports of consulting agencies under the Fish and Wildlife Coordination Act, 16 U.S.C. 661 et seq., and the National Historic Preservation Act of 1966, 16 U.S.C. 470 et seq., where such consultation has taken place. In the case of documents not likely to be easily accessible (such as inter.   tudies or reports), the agency should indicate how such information may be obtained. If such information is attached to the statement, care should be taken to ensure that the statement remains an essentially self-contained instrument, capable of being understood by the reader without the need for undue cross reference.

87

(c) Each environmental statement should be prepared in accordance with the precept in section 102(2)(A) of the Act that all agencies of the Federal Government "utilize a systematic, interdisciplinary approach which will insure the integrated use of the natural and social sciences and the environmental design arts in planning and decisionmaking which may have an impact on man's environment." Agencies should attempt to have relevant disciplines represented on their own staffs; where this is not feasible they should make appropriate use of relevant Federal, State, and local agencies or the professional services of universities and outside consultants. The interdisciplinary approach should not be limited to the preparation of the environmental impact statement, but should also be used in the early planning stages of the proposed action. Early application of such an approach should help assure a systematic evaluation of reasonable alternative courses of action and their potential social, economic, and environmental consequences.

(d) Appendix I prescribes the form of the summary sheet which should accompany each draft and final environmental statement.

§ 1500.9 Review of draft environmental statements by Federal, Federal-State, State, and local agencies and by the public.

(a) *Federal agency review.* (1) *In general.* A Federal agency considering an action requiring an environmental statement should consult with, and (on the basis of a draft environmental statement for which the agency takes responsibility) obtain the comment on the environmental impact of the action of Federal and Federal-State agencies with jurisdiction by law or special expertise with respect to any environmental impact involved. These Federal and Federal-State agencies and their relevant areas of expertise include those identified in Appendices II and III to these guidelines. It is recommended that the listed departments and agencies establish contact points, which may be regional offices, for providing comments on the environmental statements. The requirement in section 102(2)(C) to obtain comment from Federal agencies having jurisdiction or special expertise is in addition to any specific statutory obligation of any Federal agency to coordinate or consult with any other Federal or State agency. Agencies should, for example, be alert to consultation requirements of the Fish and Wildlife Co-

ordination Act, 16 U.S.C. 661 et seq., and the National Historic Preservation Act of 1966, 16 U.S.C. 470 et seq. To the extent possible, statements or finding concerning environmental impact required by other statutes, such as section 4(f) of the Department of Transportation Act of 1966, 49 U.S.C. 1653(f); or section 106 of the National Historic Preservation Act of 1966, should be combined with compliance with the environmental impact statement requirements of section 102(2)(C) of the Act to yield a single document which meets all applicable requirements. The Advisory Council on Historic Preservation, the Department of Transportation, and the Department of the Interior, in consultation with the Council, will issue any necessary supplementing instructions for furnishing information or findings not forthcoming under the environmental impact statement process.

(b) *EPA review.* Section 309 of the Clean Air Act, as amended (42 U.S.C. § 1857h-7), provides that the Administrator of the Environmental Protection Agency shall comment in writing on the environmental impact of any matter relating to his duties and responsibilities, and shall refer to the Council any matter that the Administrator determines is unsatisfactory from the standpoint of public health or welfare or environmental quality. Accordingly, wherever an agency action related to air or water quality, noise abatement and control, pesticide regulation, solid waste disposal, generally applicable environmental radiation criteria and standards, or other provision of the authority of the Administrator is involved, Federal agencies are required to submit such proposed actions and their environmental impact statements, if such have been prepared, to the Administrator for review and comment in writing. In all cases where EPA determines that proposed agency action is environmentally unsatisfactory, or where EPA determines that an environmental statement is so inadequate that such a determination cannot be made, EPA shall publish its determination and notify the Council as soon as practicable. The Administrator's comments shall constitute his comments for the purposes of both section 309 of the Clean Air Act and section 102(2)(C) of the National Environmental Policy Act.

(c) State and local review. Office of Management and Budget Circular No. A-95 (Revised) through its system of State and areawide clearinghouses provides a means for securing the views of

which can assist in the preparation and review of environmental impact statements. Current instructions for obtaining the views of such agencies are contained in the joint OMB–CEQ memorandum attached to these guidelines as Appendix IV. A current listing of clearinghouses is issued periodically by the Office of Management and Budget.

(d) *Public review:* The procedures established by these guidelines are designed to encourage public participation in the impact statement process at the earliest possible time. Agency procedures should make provision for facilitating the comment of public and private organizations and individuals by announcing the availability of draft environmental statements and by making copies available to organizations and individuals that request an opportunity to comment. Agencies should devise methods for publicizing the existence of draft statements, for example, by publication of notices in local newspapers or by maintaining a list of groups, including relevant conservation commissions, known to be interested in the agency's activities and directly notifying such groups of the existence of a draft statement, or sending them a copy, as soon as it has been prepared. A copy of the draft statement should in all cases be sent to any applicant whose project is the subject of the statement. Materials to be made available to the public shall be provided without charge to the extent practicable, or at a fee which is not more than the actual cost of reproducing copies required to be sent to other Federal agencies, including the Council.

(e) *Responsibilities of commenting entities.* (1) Agencies and members of the public submitting comments on proposed actions on the basis of draft environmental statements should endeavor to make their comments as specific, substantive, and factual as possible without undue attention to matters of form in the impact statement. Although the comments need not conform to any particular format, it would assist agencies reviewing comments if the comments were organized in a manner consistent with the structure of the draft statement. Emphasis should be placed on the assessment of the environmental impacts of the proposed action, and the acceptability of those impacts on the quality of the environment, particularly as contrasted with the impacts of reasonable alternatives to the action. Commenting entities may recommend modifications to the proposed action and/or new alternatives

that will enhance environmental quality and avoid or minimize adverse environmental impacts.

(2) Commenting agencies should indicate whether any of their projects not identified in the draft statement are sufficiently advanced in planning and related environmentally to the proposed action so that a discussion of the environmental interrelationships should be included in the final statement (see § 1500.8(a)(1)). The Council is available to assist agencies in making such determinations.

(3) Agencies and members of the public should indicate in their comments the nature of any monitoring of the environmental effects of the proposed project that appears particularly appropriate. Such monitoring may be necessary during the construction, startup, or operation phases of the project. Agencies with special expertise with respect to the environmental impacts involved are encouraged to assist the sponsoring agency in the establishment and operation of appropriate environmental monitoring.

(f) Agencies seeking comment shall establish time limits of not less than forty-five (45) days for reply, after which it may be presumed, unless the agency or party consulted requests a specified extension of time, that the agency or party consulted has no comment to make. Agencies seeking comment should endeavor to comply with requests for extensions of time of up to fifteen (15) days. In determining an appropriate period for comment, agencies should consider the magnitude and complexity of the statement and the extent of citizen interest in the proposed action.

§ 1500.10 Preparation and circulation of final environmental statements.

(a) Agencies should make every effort to discover and discuss all major points of view on the environmental effects of the proposed action and its alternatives in the draft statement itself. However, where opposing professional views and responsible opinion have been overlooked in the draft statement and are brought to the agency's attention through the commenting process, the agency should review the environmental effects of the action in light of those views and should make a meaningful reference in the final statement to the existence of any responsible opposing view not adequately discussed in the draft statement, indicating the agency's response to the issues raised. All substantive comments received on the draft (or summaries thereof where response has been exceptionally voluminous) should be attached to the final statement, whether or not each such statement is thought to merit individual discussion by the agency in the text of the statement.

(b) Copies of final statements, with comments attached, shall be sent to all Federal, State, and local agencies and private organizations that made substantive comments on the draft statement and to individuals who requested a copy of the final statement, as well as any applicant whose project is the subject of the statement. Copies of final statements shall in all cases be sent to the Environmental Protection Agency to assist it in carrying out its responsibilities under section 309 of the Clean Air Act. Where the number of comments on a draft statement is such that distribution of the final statement to all commenting entities appears impracticable, the agency shall consult with the Council concerning alternative arrangements for distribution of the statement.

§ 1500.11 Transmittal of statements to the Council; minimum periods for review; requests by the Council.

(a) As soon as they have been prepared, ten (10) copies of draft environmental statements, five (5) copies of all comments made thereon (to be forwarded to the Council by the entity making comment at the time comment is forwarded to the responsible agency), and ten (10) copies of the final text of environmental statements (together with the substance of all comments received by the responsible agency from Federal, State, and local agencies and from private organizations and individuals) shall be supplied to the Council. This will serve to meet the statutory requirement to make environmental statements available to the President. At the same time that copies of draft and final statements are sent to the Council, copies should also be sent to relevant commenting entities as set forth in §§ 1500.9 and 1500.10(b) of these guidelines.

(b) To the maximum extent practicable no administrative action subject to section 102(2) (C) is to be taken sooner than ninety (90) days after a draft environmental statement has been circulated for comment, furnished to the Council and, except where advance public disclosure will result in significantly increased costs of procurement to the Government, made available to the public pursuant to these guidelines; neither should such administrative action be taken sooner than thirty (30) days after the final text of an environmental state-

ment (together with comments) has been made available to the Council, commenting agencies, and the public. In all cases, agencies should allot a sufficient review period for the final statement so as to comply with the statutory requirement that the "statement and the comments and views of appropriate Federal, State, and local agencies * * * accompany the proposal through the existing agency review processes." If the final text of an environmental statement is filed within ninety (90) days after a draft statement has been circulated for comment, furnished to the Council and made public pursuant to this section of these guidelines, the minimum thirty (30) day period and the ninety (90) day period may run concurrently to the extent that they overlap. An agency may at any time supplement or amend a draft or final environmental statement, particularly when substantial changes are made in the proposed action, or significant new information becomes available concerning its environmental aspects. In such cases the agency should consult with the Council with respect to the possible need for or desirability of recirculation of the statement for the appropriate period.

(c) The Council will publish weekly in the FEDERAL REGISTER lists of environmental statements received during the preceding week that are available for public comment. The date of publication of such lists shall be the date from which the minimum periods for review and advance availability of statements shall be calculated.

(d) The Council's publication of notice of the availability of statements is in addition to the agency's responsibility, as described in § 1500.9(d) of these guidelines, to insure the fullest practicable provision of timely public information concerning the existence and availability of environmental statements. The agency responsible for the environmental statement is also responsible for making the statement, the comments received, and any underlying documents available to the public pursuant to the provisions of the Freedom of Information Act (5 U.S.C., 552), without regard to the exclusion of intra- or interagency memoranda when such memoranda transmit comments of Federal agencies on the environmental impact of the proposed action pursuant to § 1500.9 of these guidelines. Agency procedures prepared pursuant to § 1500.3(a) of these guidelines shall implement these public information requirements and shall include arrangements for availability of

ments at the head and appropriate regional offices of the responsible agency and at appropriate State and areawide clearinghouses unless the Governor of the State involved designates to the Council some other point for receipt of this information. Notice of such designation of an alternate point for receipt of this information will be included in the Office of Management and Budget listing of clearinghouses referred to in § 1500.9(c).

(e) Where emergency circumstances make it necessary to take an action with significant environmental impact without observing the provisions of these guidelines concerning minimum periods for agency review and advance availability of environmental statements, the Federal agency proposing to take the action should consult with the Council about alternative arrangements. Similarly where there are overriding considerations of expense to the Government or impaired program effectiveness, the responsible agency should consult with the Council concerning appropriate modifications of the minimum periods.

(f) In order to assist the Council in fulfilling its responsibilities under the Act and under Executive Order 11514, all agencies shall (as required by section 102(2)(H) of the Act and section 3(i) of Executive Order 11514) be responsive to requests by the Council for reports and other information dealing with issues arising in connection with the implementation of the Act. In particular, agencies shall be responsive to a request by the Council for the preparation and circulation of an environmental statement, unless the agency determines that such a statement is not required, in which case the agency shall prepare an environmental assessment and a publicly available record briefly setting forth the reasons for its determination. In no case, however, shall the Council's silence or failure to comment or request preparation, modification, or recirculation of an environmental statement or to take other action with respect to an environmental statement be construed as bearing in any way on the question of the legal requirement for or the adequacy of such statement under the Act.

§ 1500.12 Legislative actions.

(a) The Council and the Office of Management and Budget will cooperate in giving guidance as needed to assist agencies in identifying legislative items believed to have environmental significance. Agencies should prepare impact legislative proposals to the Office of Management and Budget. In this regard, agencies should identify types of repetitive legislation requiring environmental impact statements (such as certain types of bills affecting transportation policy or annual construction authorizations).

(b) With respect to recommendations or reports on proposals for legislation to which section 102(2)(C) applies, the final text of the environmental statement and comments thereon should be available to the Congress and to the public for consideration in connection with the proposed legislation or report. In cases where the scheduling of congressional hearings on recommendations or reports on proposals for legislation which the Federal agency has forwarded to the Congress does not allow adequate time for the completion of a final text of an environmental statement (together with comments), a draft environmental statement may be furnished to the Congress and made available to the public pending transmittal of the comments as received and the final text.

§ 1500.13 Application of section 102 (2)(C) procedure to existing projects and programs.

Agencies have an obligation to reassess ongoing projects and programs in order to avoid or minimize adverse environmental effects. The section 102(2)(C) procedure shall be applied to further major Federal actions having a significant effect on the environment even though they arise from projects or programs initiated prior to enactment of the Act on January 1, 1970. While the status of the work and degree of completion may be considered in determining whether to proceed with the project, it is essential that the environmental impacts of proceeding are reassessed pursuant to the Act's policies and procedures and, if the project or program is continued, that further incremental major actions be shaped so as to enhance and restore environmental quality as well as to avoid or minimize adverse environmental consequences. It is also important in further action that account be taken of environmental consequences not fully evaluated at the outset of the project or program.

§ 1500.14 Supplementary guidelines; evaluation of procedures.

(a) The Council after examining environmental statements and agency procedures with respect to such statements will issue such supplements to these guidelines as are necessary.

their experience in the implementation of the section 102(2)(C) provisions of the Act and in conforming with these guidelines and report thereon to the Council by June 30, 1974. Such reports should include an identification of the problem areas and suggestions for revision or clarification of these guidelines to achieve effective coordination of views on environmental aspects (and alternatives, where appropriate) of proposed actions without imposing unproductive administrative procedures. Such reports shall also indicate what progress the agency has made in developing substantive criteria and guidance for making environmental assessments as required by § 1500.6(c) of this directive and by section 102(2)(B) of the Act.

Effective date. The revisions of these guidelines shall apply to all draft and final impact statements filed with the Council after January 28, 1974.

RUSSELL E. TRAIN,
Chairman.

APPENDIX I—SUMMARY TO ACCOMPANY DRAFT AND FINAL STATEMENTS

(Check one) ( ) Draft. ( ) Final Environmental Statement.

Name of responsible Federal agency (with name of operating division where appropriate). Name, address, and telephone number of individual at the agency who can be contacted for additional information about the proposed action or the statement.

1. Name of action (Check one) ( ) Administrative Action. ( ) Legislative Action.

2. Brief description of action and its purpose. Indicate what States (and counties) particularly affected, and what other proposed Federal actions in the area, if any, are discussed in the statement.

3. Summary of environmental impacts and adverse environmental effects.

4. Summary of major alternatives considered.

5. (For draft statements) List all Federal, State, and local agencies and other parties from which comments have been requested. (For final statements) List all Federal, State, and local agencies and other parties from which written comments have been received.

6. Date draft statement (and final environmental statement, if one has been issued) made available to the Council and the public.

APPENDIX II—AREAS OF ENVIRONMENTAL IMPACT AND FEDERAL AGENCIES AND FEDERAL STATE AGENCIES [1] WITH JURISDICTION BY LAW OR SPECIAL EXPERTISE TO COMMENT THEREON [2]

AIR

Air Quality

Department of Agriculture—
Forest Service (effects on vegetation)

stances)
Department of Health, Education, and Welfare
Environmental Protection Agency
Department of the Interior—
Bureau of Mines (fossil and gaseous fuel combustion)
Bureau of Sport Fisheries and Wildlife (effect on wildlife)
Bureau of Outdoor Recreation (effects on recreation)
Bureau of Land Management (public lands)
Bureau of Indian Affairs (Indian lands)
National Aeronautics and Space Administration (remote sensing, aircraft emissions)
Department of Transportation—
Assistant Secretary for Systems Development and Technology (auto emissions)
Coast Guard (vessel emissions)
Federal Aviation Administration (aircraft emissions)

Weather Modification

Department of Agriculture—
Forest Service
Department of Commerce—
National Oceanic and Atmospheric Administration
Department of Defense—
Department of the Air Force
Department of the Interior
Bureau of Reclamation

WATER RESOURCES COUNCIL

WATER

Water Quality

Department of Agriculture—
Soil Conservation Service
Forest Service
Atomic Energy Commission (radioactive substances)
Department of the Interior—
Bureau of Reclamation
Bureau of Land Management (public lands)
Bureau of Indian Affairs (Indian lands)
Bureau of Sports Fisheries and Wildlife
Bureau of Outdoor Recreation
Geological Survey
Office of Saline Water
Environmental Protection Agency
Department of Health, Education, and Welfare

---

[1] River Basin Commissions (Delaware, Great Lakes, Missouri, New England, Ohio, Pacific Northwest, Souris-Red-Rainy, Susquehanna, Upper Mississippi) and similar Federal-State agencies should be consulted on actions affecting the environment of their specific geographic jurisdictions.

[2] In all cases where a proposed action will have significant international environmental effects, the Department of State should be consulted, and should be sent a copy of any draft and final impact statement which covers such action.

Department of Defense—
  Army Corps of Engineers
  Department of the Navy (ship pollution control)
National Aeronautics and Space Administration (remote sensing)
Department of Transportation—
  Coast Guard (oil spills, ship sanitation)
Department of Commerce—
  National Oceanic and Atmospheric Administration
Water Resources Council
River Basin Commissions (as geographically appropriate)

Marine Pollution, Commercial Fishery Conservation, and Shellfish Sanitation

Department of Commerce—
  National Oceanic and Atmospheric Administration
Department of Defense—
  Army Corps of Engineers
  Office of the Oceanographer of the Navy
Department of Health, Education, and Welfare
Department of the Interior—
  Bureau of Sport Fisheries and Wildlife
  Bureau of Outdoor Recreation
  Bureau of Land Management (outer continental shelf)
  Geological Survey (outer continental shelf)
Department of Transportation—
  Coast Guard
Environmental Protection Agency
National Aeronautics and Space Administration (remote sensing)
Water Resources Council
River Basin Commissions (as geographically appropriate)

Waterway Regulation and Stream Modification

Department of Agriculture—
  Soil Conservation Service
Department of Defense—
  Army Corps of Engineers
Department of the Interior—
  Bureau of Reclamation
  Bureau of Sport Fisheries and Wildlife
  Bureau of Outdoor Recreation
  Geological Survey
Department of Transportation—
  Coast Guard
Environmental Protection Agency
National Aeronautics and Space Administration (remote sensing)
Water Resources Council
River Basin Commissions (as geographically appropriate)

FISH AND WILDLIFE

Department of Agriculture—
  Forest Service
  Soil Conservation Service
Department of Commerce—
  National Oceanic and Atmospheric Administration (marine species)
Department of the Interior—
  Bureau of Sport Fisheries and Wildlife
  Bureau of Land Management
  Bureau of Outdoor Recreation
Environmental Protection Agency

SOLID WASTE

Atomic Energy Commission (radioactive waste)
Department of Defense—
  Army Corps of Engineers
Department of Health, Education, and Welfare
Department of the Interior—
  Bureau of Mines (mineral waste, mine acid waste, municipal solid waste, recycling)
  Bureau of Land Management (public lands)
  Bureau of Indian Affairs (Indian lands)
  Geological Survey (geologic and hydrologic effects)
  Office of Saline Water (demineralization)
Department of Transportation—
  Coast Guard (ship sanitation)
Environmental Protection Agency
River Basin Commissions (as geographically appropriate)
Water Resources Council

NOISE

Department of Commerce—
  National Bureau of Standards
Department of Health, Education, and Welfare
Department of Housing and Urban Development (land use and building materials aspects)
Department of Labor—
  Occupational Safety and Health Administration
Department of Transportation—
  Assistant Secretary for Systems Development and Technology
  Federal Aviation Administration, Office of Noise Abatement
Environmental Protection Agency
National Aeronautics and Space Administration

RADIATION

Atomic Energy Commission
Department of Commerce—
  National Bureau of Standards
Department of Health, Education, and Welfare
Department of the Interior—
  Bureau of Mines (uranium mines)
  Mining Enforcement and Safety Administration (uranium mines)
Environmental Protection Agency

HAZARDOUS SUBSTANCES
Toxic Materials

Atomic Energy Commission (radioactive substances)
Department of Agriculture—
  Agricultural Research Service
  Consumer and Marketing Service
Department of Commerce—
  National Oceanic and Atmospheric Administration
Department of Defense
Department of Health, Education, and Welfare
Environmental Protection Agency

Food Additives and Contamination of Foodstuffs

Department of Agriculture—
Consumer and Marketing Service (meat and poultry products)
Department of Health, Education, and Welfare
Environmental Protection Agency

Pesticides

Department of Agriculture—
Agricultural Research Service (biological controls, food and fiber production)
Consumer and Marketing Service
Forest Service
Department of Commerce—
National Oceanic and Atmospheric Administration
Department of Health, Education, and Welfare
Department of the Interior—
Bureau of Sport Fisheries and Wildlife (fish and wildlife effects)
Bureau of Land Management (public lands)
Bureau of Indian Affairs (Indian lands)
Bureau of Reclamation (irrigated lands)
Environmental Protection Agency

Transportation and Handling of Hazardous Materials

Atomic Energy Commission (radioactive substances)
Department of Commerce—
Maritime Administration
National Oceanic and Atmospheric Administration (effects on marine life and the coastal zone)
Department of Defense—
Armed Services Explosive Safety Board
Army Corps of Engineers (navigable waterways)
Department of Transportation—
Federal Highway Administration, Bureau of Motor Carrier Safety
Coast Guard
Federal Railroad Administration
Federal Aviation Administration
Assistant Secretary for Systems Development and Technology
Office of Hazardous Materials
Office of Pipeline Safety
Environmental Protection Agency

ENERGY SUPPLY AND NATURAL RESOURCES DEVELOPMENT

Electric Energy Development, Generation, and Transmission, and Use

Atomic Energy Commission (nuclear)
Department of Agriculture—
Rural Electrification Administration (rural areas)
Department of Defense—
Army Corps of Engineers (hydro)
Department of Health, Education, and Welfare (radiation effects)
Department of Housing and Urban Development (urban areas)
Department of the Interior—
Bureau of Indian Affairs (Indian lands)
Bureau of Land Management (public lands)
Bureau of Reclamation
Power Marketing Administrations
Geological Survey
Bureau of Sport Fisheries and Wildlife
Bureau of Outdoor Recreation
National Park Service
Environmental Protection Agency
Federal Power Commission (hydro, transmission, and supply)
River Basin Commissions (as geographically appropriate)
Tennessee Valley Authority
Water Resources Council

Petroleum Development, Extraction, Refining, Transport, and Use

Department of the Interior—
Office of Oil and Gas
Bureau of Mines
Geological Survey
Bureau of Land Management (public lands and outer continental shelf)
Bureau of Indian Affairs (Indian lands)
Bureau of Sport Fisheries and Wildlife (effects on fish and wildlife)
Bureau of Outdoor Recreation
National Park Service
Department of Transportation (Transport and Pipeline Safety)
Environmental Protection Agency
Interstate Commerce Commission

Natural Gas Development, Production, Transmission, and Use

Department of Housing and Urban Development (urban areas)
Department of the Interior—
Office of Oil and Gas
Geological Survey
Bureau of Mines
Bureau of Land Management (public lands)
Bureau of Indian Affairs (Indian lands)
Bureau of Sport Fisheries and Wildlife
Bureau of Outdoor Recreation
National Park Service
Department of Transportation (transport and safety)
Environmental Protection Agency
Federal Power Commission (production, transmission, and supply)
Interstate Commerce Commission

Coal and Minerals Development, Mining, Conversion, Processing, Transport, and Use

Appalachian Regional Commission
Department of Agriculture—
Forest Service
Department of Commerce
Department of the Interior—
Office of Coal Research
Mining Enforcement and Safety Administration
Bureau of Mines
Geological Survey
Bureau of Indian Affairs (Indian lands)
Bureau of Land Management (public lands)
Bureau of Sport Fisheries and Wildlife
Bureau of Outdoor Recreation
National Park Service

Occupational Safety and Health Administration
Department of Transportation
Environmental Protection Agency
Interstate Commerce Commission
Tennessee Valley Authority

Renewable Resource Development, Production, Management, Harvest, Transport, and Use

Department of Agriculture—
  Forest Service
  Soil Conservation Service
Department of Commerce
Department of Housing and Urban Development (building materials)
Department of the Interior—
  Geological Survey
  Bureau of Land Management (public lands)
  Bureau of Indian Affairs (Indian lands)
  Bureau of Sport Fisheries and Wildlife
  Bureau of Outdoor Recreation
  National Park Service
Department of Transportation
Environmental Protection Agency
Interstate Commerce Commission (freight rates)

Energy and Natural Resources Conservation

Department of Agriculture—
  Forest Service
  Soil Conservation Service
Department of Commerce—
  National Bureau of Standards (energy efficiency)
Department of Housing and Urban Development—
  Federal Housing Administration (housing standards)
Department of the Interior—
  Office of Energy Conservation
  Bureau of Mines
  Bureau of Reclamation
  Geological Survey
  Power Marketing Administration
Department of Transportation
Environmental Protection Agency
Federal Power Commission
General Services Administration (design and operation of buildings)
Tennessee Valley Authority

LAND USE AND MANAGEMENT

Land Use Changes, Planning and Regulation of Land Development

Department of Agriculture—
  Forest Service (forest lands)
  Agricultural Research Service (agricultural lands)
Department of Housing and Urban Development
Department of the Interior—
  Office of Land Use and Water Planning
  Bureau of Land Management (public la
  Bureau of Land Management (public lands)
  Bureau of Indian Affairs (Indian lands)
  Bureau of Sport Fisheries and Wildlife (wildlife refuges)

lands)
  National Park Service (NPS units)
Department of Transportation
Environmental Protection Agency (pollution effects)
National Aeronautics and Space Administration (remote sensing)
River Basins Commissions (as geographically appropriate).

Public Land Management

Department of Agriculture—
  Forest Service (forests)
Department of Defense
Department of the Interior—
  Bureau of Land Management
  Bureau of Indian Affairs (Indian lands)
  Bureau of Sport Fisheries and Wildlife (wildlife refuges)
  Bureau of Outdoor Recreation (recreation lands)
  National Park Service (NPS units)
Federal Power Commission (project lands)
General Services Administration
National Aeronautics and Space Administration (remote sensing)
Tennessee Valley Authority (project lands)

PROTECTION OF ENVIRONMENTALLY CRITICAL AREAS—FLOODPLAINS, WETLANDS, BEACHES AND DUNES, UNSTABLE SOILS, STEEP SLOPES, AQUIFER RECHARGE AREAS, ETC.

Department of Agriculture—
  Agricultural Stabilization and Conservation Service
  Soil Conservation Service
  Forest Service
Department of Commerce—
  National Oceanic and Atmospheric Administration (coastal areas)
Department of Defense—
  Army Corps of Engineers
Department of Housing and Urban Development (urban and floodplain areas)
Department of the Interior—
  Office of Land Use and Water Planning
  Bureau of Outdoor Recreation
  Bureau of Reclamation
  Bureau of Sport Fisheries and Wildlife
  Bureau of Land Management
  Geological Survey
Environmental Protection Agency (pollution effects)
National Aeronautics and Space Administration (remote sensing)
River Basins Commissions (as geographically appropriate)
Water Resources Council

LAND USE IN COASTAL AREAS

Department of Agriculture—
  Forest Service
  Soil Conservation Service (soil stability, hydrology)
Department of Commerce—
  National Oceanic and Atmospheric Administration (impact on marine life and coastal zone management)
Department of Defense—
  Army Corps of Engineers (beaches, dredg' and fill permits, Refuse Act permits)
Department of Housing and Urban Development (urban areas)

Office of Land Use and Water Planning
Bureau of Sport Fisheries and Wildlife
National Park Service
Geological Survey
Bureau of Outdoor Recreation
Bureau of Land Management (public lands)
Department of Transportation—
Coast Guard (bridges, navigation)
Environmental Protection Agency (pollution effects)
National Aeronautics and Space Administration (remote sensing)

REDEVELOPMENT AND CONSTRUCTION IN BUILT-UP AREAS

Department of Commerce—
Economic Development Administration (designated areas)
Department of Housing and Urban Development
Department of the Interior—
Office of Land Use and Water Planning
Department of Transportation
Environmental Protection Agency
General Services Administration
Office of Economic Opportunity

DENSITY AND CONGESTION MITIGATION

Department of Health, Education, and Welfare
Department of Housing and Urban Development
Department of the Interior—
Office of Land Use and Water Planning
Bureau of Outdoor Recreation
Department of Transportation
Environmental Protection Agency

NEIGHBORHOOD CHARACTER AND CONTINUITY

Department of Health, Education, and Welfare
Department of Housing and Urban Development
National Endowment for the Arts
Office of Economic Opportunity

IMPACTS ON LOW-INCOME POPULATIONS

Department of Commerce—
Economic Development Administration (designated areas)
Department of Health, Education, and Welfare
Department of Housing and Urban Development
Office of Economic Opportunity

HISTORIC, ARCHITECTURAL, AND ARCHEOLOGICAL PRESERVATION

Advisory Council on Historic Preservation
Department of Housing and Urban Development
Department of the Interior—
National Park Service
Bureau of Land Management (public lands)
Bureau of Indian Affairs (Indian lands)
General Services Administration
National Endowment for the Arts

HYDROLOGY

Department of Agriculture—
Soil Conservation Service
Agricultural Service
Forest Service
Department of Commerce—
National Oceanic and Atmospheric Administration
Department of Defense—
Army Corps of Engineers (dredging, aquatic plants)
Department of Health, Education, and Welfare
Department of the Interior—
Bureau of Land Management
Bureau of Sport Fisheries and Wildlife
Geological Survey
Bureau of Reclamation
Environmental Protection Agency
National Aeronautics and Space Administration (remote sensing)
River Basin Commissions (as geographically appropriate)
Water Resources Council

OUTDOOR RECREATION

Department of Agriculture—
Forest Service
Soil Conservation Service
Department of Defense—
Army Corps of Engineers
Department of Housing and Urban Development (urban areas)
Department of the Interior—
Bureau of Land Management
National Park Service
Bureau of Outdoor Recreation
Bureau of Sport Fisheries and Wildlife
Bureau of Indian Affairs
Environmental Protection Agency
National Aeronautics and Space Administration (remote sensing)
River Basin Commissions (as geographically appropriate)
Water Resources Council

APPENDIX III—OFFICES WITHIN FEDERAL AGENCIES AND FEDERAL-STATE AGENCIES FOR INFORMATION REGARDING THE AGENCIES' NEPA ACTIVITIES AND FOR RECEIVING OTHER AGENCIES' IMPACT STATEMENTS FOR WHICH COMMENTS ARE REQUESTED

ADVISORY COUNCIL ON HISTORIC PRESERVATION

Office of Architectural and Environmental Preservation, Advisory Council on Historic Preservation, Suite 430, 1522 K Street N.W., Washington, D.C. 20005 254–3974

DEPARTMENT OF AGRICULTURE

Office of the Secretary, Attn: Coordinator Environmental Quality Activities, U.S. Department of Agriculture, Washington, D.C. 20250 447–3965

---

[1] Requests for comments or information from individual units of the Department of Agriculture, e.g., Soil Conservation Service, Forest Service, etc. should be sent to the Office of the Secretary, Department of Agriculture, at the address given above.

Office of the Alternate Federal Co-Chairman, Appalachian Regional Commission, 1666 Connecticut Avenue, N.W., Washington, D.C. 20235 967–4103

DEPARTMENT OF THE ARMY (CORPS OF ENGINEERS)

Executive Director of Civil Works, Office of the Chief of Engineers, U.S. Army Corps of Engineers, Washington, D.C. 20314 693–7168

ATOMIC ENERGY COMMISSION

For nonregulatory matters: Office of Assistant General Manager for Biomedical and Environmental Research and Safety Programs, Atomic Energy Commission, Washington, D.C. 20545 973–3208
For regulatory matters: Office of the Assistant Director for Environmental Projects, Atomic Energy Commission, Washington, D.C. 20545 973–7531

DEPARTMENT OF COMMERCE

Office of the Deputy Assistant Secretary for Environmental Affairs, U.S. Department of Commerce, Washington, D.C. 20230 967–4335

DEPARTMENT OF DEFENSE

Office of the Assistant Secretary for Defense (Health and Environment), U.S. Department of Defense, Room 3E172, The Pentagon, Washington, D.C. 20301 697-2111

DELAWARE RIVER BASIN COMMISSION

Office of the Secretary, Delaware River Basin Commission, Post Office Box 360, Trenton, N.J. 08603 (609) 883-9500

ENVIRONMENTAL PROTECTION AGENCY [2]

Director, Office of Federal Activities, Environmental Protection Agency, 401 M Street, S.W., Washington, D.C. 20460 755–0777

---

[2] Contact the Office of Federal Activities for environmental statements concerning legislation, regulations, national program proposals or other major policy issues.
For all other EPA consultation, contact the Regional Administrator in whose area the proposed action (e.g., highway or water resource construction projects) will take place. The Regional Administrators will coordinate the EPA review. Addresses of the Regional Administrators, and the areas covered by their regions are as follows:

Regional Administrator, I,
U.S. Environmental Protection Agency
Room 2303, John F. Kennedy
Federal Bldg., Boston, Mass. 02203,
(617) 223–7210

Connecticut, Maine, Massachusetts, New Hampshire, Rhode Island, Vermont

Regional Administrator, II,
U.S. Environmental Protection Agency
Room 908, 26 Federal Plaza
New York, New York 10007
(212) 264-2525

New Jersey, New York, Puerto Rico, Virgin Islands

Regional Administrator, III,
U.S. Environmental Protection Agency
Curtis Bldg., 6th & Walnut Sts.
Philadelphia, Pa. 19106
(215) 597-9801

Delaware, Maryland, Pennsylvania, Virginia, West Virginia, District of Columbia

Regional Administrator, IV,
U.S. Environmental Protection Agency
1421 Peachtree Street
N.E., Atlanta, Ga. 30309
(404) 526–5727

Alabama, Florida, Georgia, Kentucky Mississippi, North Carolina, South Carolina, Tennessee

Regional Administrator V,
U.S. Environmental Protection Agency
1 N. Wacker Drive
Chicago, Illinois 60606
(312) 353–5250

Illinois, Indiana, Michigan, Minnesota, Ohio, Wisconsin

Regional Administrator VI,
U.S. Environmental Protection Agency
1600 Patterson Street
Suite 1100
Dallas, Texas 75201
(214) 749–1962

Arkansas, Louisiana, New Mexico, Texas, Oklahoma

Regional Administrator VII,
U.S. Environmental Protection Agency
1735 Baltimore Avenue
Kansas City, Missouri 64108
(816) 374–5493

Iowa, Kansas, Missouri, Nebraska

Commission's Advisor on Environmental Quality, Federal Power Commission, 825 N. Capitol Street, N.E., Washington, D.C. 20426 386-6084

GENERAL SERVICES ADMINISTRATION

Office of Environmental Affairs, Office of the Deputy Administrator for Special Projects, General Services Administration, Washington, D.C. 20405 343-4161

Office of the Chairman, Great Lakes Basin Commission, 3475 Plymouth Road, P.O. Box 999, Ann Arbor, Michigan 48105 (313) 76- 7431

DEPARTMENT OF HEALTH, EDUCATION AND WELFARE [3]

Office of Environmental Affairs, Office of the Assistant Secretary for Administration and Management, Department of Health, Education and Welfare, Washington, D.C. 20201 963-4456

Regional Administrator VIII,
U.S. Environmental Protection Agency
Suite 900, Lincoln Tower
1860 Lincoln Street
Denver, Colorado 80203
(303) 837-3895

Colorado, Montana, North Dakota, South Dakota, Utah, Wyoming

Regional Administrator IX,
U.S. Environmental Protection Agency
100 California Street
San Francisco, California 94111
(415) 556-2320

Arizona, California, Hawaii, Nevada, American Samoa, Guam, Trust Territories of Pacific Islands, Wake Island

Regional Administrator X,
U.S. Environmental Protection Agency
1200 Sixth Avenue
Seattle, Washington 98101
(206) 442-1220

Alaska, Idaho, Oregon, Washington

[3] Contact the Office of Environmental Affairs for information on HEW's environmental statements concerning legislation, regulations, national program proposals or other major policy issues, and for all requests for HEW comment on impact statements of other agencies.

For information with respect to HEW actions occurring within the jurisdiction of the Departments' Regional Directors, contact the appropriate Regional Environmental Officer:

Region I:
Regional Environmental Officer
U.S. Department of Health, Education and Welfare
Room 2007B
John F. Kennedy Center
Boston, Massachusetts 02203 (617) 223-6837

Region II:
Regional Environmental Officer
U.S. Department of Health, Education and Welfare
Federal Building
26 Federal Plaza
New York, New York 10007 (212) 264-1308

Region III:
Regional Environmental Officer
U.S. Department of Health, Education and Welfare
P.O. Box 13716
Philadelphia, Pennsylvania 19101 (215) 597-6498

Region IV:
Regional Environmental Officer
U.S. Department of Health, Education and Welfare
Room 404
50 Seventh Street, N.E.
Atlanta, Georgia 30323 (404) 526-5817

Region V:
Regional Environmental Officer
U.S. Department of Health, Education and Welfare
Room 712, New Post Office Building
433 West Van Buren Street
Chicago, Illinois 60607 (312) 353-1644

Region VI:
Regional Environmental Officer
U.S. Department of Health, Education and Welfare
1114 Commerce Street
Dallas, Texas 75202 (214) 749-2236

Region VII:
Regional Environmental Officer
U.S. Department of Health, Education and Welfare
601 East 12th Street
Kansas City, Missouri 64106 (816) 374-3584

Region VIII:
Regional Environmental Officer
U.S. Department of Health, Education and Welfare
9017 Federal Building
19th and Stout Streets
Denver, Colorado 80202 (303) 837-4178

Region IX:
Regional Environmental Officer
U.S. Department of Health, Education and Welfare
50 Fulton Street
San Francisco, California 94102 (415) 556-1970

Region X:
Regional Environmental Officer
U.S. Department of Health, Education and Welfare
Arcade Plaza Building
1321 Second Street
Seattle, Washington 98101 (206) 442-0490

Director, Office of Community and Environmental Standards, Department of Housing and Urban Development, Room 7206, Washington, D.C. 20410
755-5980

DEPARTMENT OF THE INTERIOR [5]

Director, Office of Environmental Project Review, Department of the Interior, Interior Building, Washington, D.C. 20240 343-3291

INTERSTATE COMMERCE COMMISSION

Office of Proceedings, Interstate Commerce, Commission, Washington, D.C. 20423
343-610

DEPARTMENT OF LABOR

Assistant Secretary for Occupational Safety and Health, Department of Labor, Washington, D.C. 20210
961-3405

MISSOURI RIVER BASINS COMMISSION

Office of the Chairman, Missouri River Basins Commission, 10050 Regency Circle, Omaha, Nebraska 68114
(402) 397-5714

SPACE ADMINISTRATION

Office of the Comptroller, National Aeronautics and Space Administration, Washington, D.C. 20546
755-8440

NATIONAL CAPITAL PLANNING COMMISSION

Office of Environmental Affairs, Office of the Executive Director, National Capital Planning Commission, Washington, D.C. 20576
382-7200

NATIONAL ENDOWMENT FOR THE ARTS

Office of Architecture and Environmental Arts Program, National Endowment for the Arts, Washington, D.C. 20506
382-5765

NEW ENGLAND RIVER BASINS COMMISSION

Office of the Chairman, New England River Basins Commission, 55 Court Street, Boston, Mass. 02108
(617) 223-6244

OFFICE OF ECONOMIC OPPORTUNITY

Office of the Director, Office of Economic Opportunity, 1200 19th Street, N.W., Washington, D.C. 20506
254-6000

---

[4] Contact the Director with regard to environmental impacts of legislation, policy statements, program regulations and procedures, and precedent-making project decisions. For all other HUD consultation, contact the HUD Regional Administrator in whose jurisdiction the project lies, as follows:

Regional Administrator I,
Environmental Clearance Officer
U.S. Department of Housing and Urban Development
Room 405, John F. Kennedy Federal Building
Boston, Mass. 02203 (617) 223-4066

Regional Administrator II,
Environmental Clearance Officer
U.S. Department of Housing and Urban Development
26 Federal Plaza
New York, New York 10007 (212) 264-8068

Regional Administrator III,
Environmental Clearance Officer
U.S. Department of Housing and Urban Development
Curtis Building, Sixth and Walnut Street
Philadelphia, Pennsylvania 19106 (215) 597-2560

Regional Administrator IV,
Environmental Clearance Officer
U.S. Department of Housing and Urban Development
Peachtree-Seventh Building
Atlanta, Georgia 30323 (404) 526-5585

Regional Administrator V,
Environmental Clearance Officer
U.S. Department of Housing and Urban Development
360 North Michigan Avenue
Chicago, Illinois 60601 (312) 353-5680

Regional Administrator VI,
Environmental Clearance Officer
U.S. Department of Housing and Urban Development
Federal Office Building, 819 Taylor Street
Fort Worth, Texas 76102 (817) 334-2867

Regional Administrator VII,
Environmental Clearance Officer
U.S. Department of Housing and Urban Development
911 Walnut Street
Kansas City, Missouri 64106 (816) 374-2661

Regional Administrator VIII,
Environmental Clearance Officer
U.S. Department of Housing and Urban Development
Samsonite Building, 1051 South Broadway
Denver, Colorado 80209 (303) 837-4061

Regional Administrator IX,
Environmental Clearance Officer
U.S. Department of Housing and Urban Development
450 Golden Gate Avenue, Post Office Box 36003
San Francisco, California 94102 (415) 556-4752

Regional Administrator X,
Environmental Clearance Officer
U.S. Department of Housing and Urban Development
Room 226, Arcade Plaza Building
Seattle, Washington 98101 (206) 583-5415

[5] Requests for comments or information from individual units of the Department of the Interior should be sent to the Office of Environmental Project Review at the address given above.

Office of the Chairman, Ohio River Basin Commission, 36 East 4th Street, Suite 208–20, Cincinnati, Ohio 45202 (513) 684–3831

PACIFIC NORTHWEST RIVER BASINS COMMISSION

Office of the Chairman, Pacific Northwest River Basins Commission, 1 Columbia River, Vancouver, Washington 98660 (206) 695–3606

SOURIS-RED-RAINY RIVER BASINS COMMISSION

Office of the Chairman, Souris-Red-Rainy River Basins Commission, Suite 6, Professional Building, Holiday Mall, Moorhead, Minnesota 56560 (701) 237–5227

DEPARTMENT OF STATE

Office of the Special Assistant to the Secretary for Environmental Affairs, Department of State, Washington, D.C. 20520 632–7964

SUSQUEHANNA RIVER BASIN COMMISSION

Office of the Executive Director, Susquehanna River Basin Commission, 5012 Lenker Street, Mechanicsburg, Pa. 17055 (717) 737–0501

TENNESSEE VALLEY AUTHORITY

Office of the Director of Environmental Research and Development, Tennessee Valley Authority, 720 Edney Building, Chattanooga, Tennessee 37401 (615) 755–2002

DEPARTMENT OF TRANSPORTATION *

Director, Office of Environmental Quality, Office of the Assistant Secretary for Environment, Safety, and Consumer Affairs, Department of Transportation, Washington, D.C. 20590 426–4357

* Contact the Office of Environmental Quality, Department of Transportation, for information on DOT's environmental statements concerning legislation, regulations, national program proposals, or other major policy issues.

For information regarding the Department of Transportation's other environmental statements, contact the national office for the appropriate administration:

U.S. Coast Guard

Office of Marine Environment and Systems, U.S. Coast Guard, 400 7th Street, S.W., Washington, D.C. 20590, 426–2007

Federal Aviation Administration

Office of Environmental Quality, Federal Aviation Administration, 800 Independence Avenue, S.W., Washington, D.C. 20591, 426–8406

Federal Highway Administration

Office of Environmental Policy, Federal Highway Administration, 400 7th Street S.W., Washington, D.C. 20590, 426–0351

Federal Railroad Administration

Office of Policy and Plans, Federal Railroad Administration, 400 7th Street, S.W., Washington, D.C. 20590, 426–1567

Urban Mass Transportation Administration

Office of Program Operations, Urban Mass Transportation Administration, 400 7th Street, S.W., Washington, D.C. 20590, 426–4020

For other administration's not listed above, contact the Office of Environmental Quality, Department of Transportation, at the address given above.

For comments on other agencies' environmental statements, contact the appropriate administration's regional office. If more than one administration within the Department of Transportation is to be requested to comment, contact the Secretarial Representative in the appropriate Regional Office for coordination of the Department's comments:

SECRETARIAL REPRESENTATIVE

Region I Secretarial Representative, U.S. Department of Transportation, Transportation Systems Center, 55 Broadway, Cambridge, Massachusetts 02142 (617) 494–2709

Region II Secretarial Representative, U.S. Department of Transportation, 26 Federal Plaza, Room 1811, New York, New York 10007 (212) 264–2672

Region III Secretarial Representative, U.S. Department of Transportation, Mail Building, Suite 1214, 325 Chestnut Street, Philadelphia, Pennsylvania 19106 (215) 597–040

Region IV Secretarial Representative, U.S. Department of Transportation, Suite 515, 1720 Peachtree Rd., N.W. Atlanta, Georgia 30309 (404) 526–3738

Region V Secretarial Representative, U.S. Department of Transportation, 17th Floor, 300 S. Wacker Drive, Chicago, Illinois 60606 (312) 353–4000

Region V Secretarial Representative, U.S. Department of Transportation, 9–C–18 Federal Center, 1100 Commerce Street, Dallas, Texas 75202 (214) 749–1851

Region VII Secretarial Representative, U.S. Department of Transportation, 601 E. 12th Street, Room 634, Kansas City, Missouri 64106 (816) 374–2761

Region VIII Secretarial Representative, U.S. Department of Transportation, Prudential Plaza, Suite 1822, 1050 17th Street, Denver, Colorado 80225 (303) 837–3242

Region IX Secretarial Representative, U.S. Department of Transportation, 450 Golden Gate Avenue, Box 36133, San Francisco California 94102 (415) 556–5961

Region X Secretarial Representative, U.S. Department of Transportation, 1321 Second Avenue, Room 507, Seattle, Washington 98101 (206) 442–0590

FEDERAL AVIATION ADMINISTRATION

New England Region, Office of the Regional Director, Federal Aviation Administration, 154 Middlesex Street, Burlington, Massachusetts 01803 (617) 272–2350

tion, Department of the Treasury, Washington, D.C. 20220 964-5391

Office of the Chairman, Upper Mississippi River Basin Commission, Federal Office Building, Fort Snelling, Twin Cities, Minnesota 55111 (612) 725-4690

sources Council, 2120 L Street, N.W., Suite 800, Washington, D.C. 20037 254-6442

APPENDIX IV—STATE AND LOCAL AGENCY
REVIEW OF IMPACT STATEMENTS

1. OMB Circular No. A-95 through its system of clearinghouses provides a means for securing the views of State and local environ-

---

Eastern Region, Office of the Regional Director, Federal Aviation Administration, Federal Building, JFK International Airport, Jamaica, New York 11430 (212) 995-3333

Southern Region, Office of the Regional Director, Federal Aviation Administration, P.O. Box 20636, Atlanta, Georgia 30320 (404) 526-7222

Great Lakes Region, Office of the Regional Director, Federal Aviation Administration, 2300 East Devon, Des Plaines, Illinois 60018 (312) 694-4500

Southwest Region, Office of the Regional Director, Federal Aviation Administration, P.O. Box 1689, Fort Worth, Texas 76101 (817) 624-4911

Central Region, Office of the Regional Director, Federal Aviation Administration, 601 E. 12th Street, Kansas City, Missouri 64106 (816) 374-5626

Rocky Mountain Region, Office of the Regional Director, Federal Aviation Administration, Park Hill Station, P.O. Box 7213, Denver, Colorado 80207 (303) 837-3646

Western Region, Office of the Regional Director, Federal Aviation Administration, P.O. Box 92007, WorldWay Postal Center, Los Angeles, California 90009 (213) 536-6427

Northwest Region, Office of the Regional Director, Federal Aviation Administration, FAA Building, Boeing Field, Seattle, Washington 98108 (206) 767-2780

FEDERAL HIGHWAY ADMINISTRATION

Region 1, Regional Administrator, Federal Highway Administration, 4 Normanskill Boulevard, Delmar, New York 12054 (518) 472-6476

Region 3, Regional Administrator, Federal Highway Administration, Room 1621, George H. Fallon Federal Office Building, 31 Hopkins Plaza, Baltimore, Maryland 21201 (301) 962-2361

Region 4, Regional Administrator, Federal Highway Administration, Suite 200, 1720 Peachtree Road, N.W., Atlanta, Georgia 30309 (404) 526-5078

Region 5, Regional Administrator, Federal Highway Administration, Dixie Highway, Homewood, Illinois 60430 (312) 799-6300

Region 6, Regional Administrator, Federal Highway Administration, 819 Taylor Street, Fort Worth, Texas 76102 (817) 334-3232

Region 7, Regional Administrator, Federal Highway Administration, P.O. Box 7186, Country Club Station, Kansas City, Missouri 64113 (816) 361-7563

Region 8, Regional Administrator, Federal Highway Administration, Room 242, Building 40, Denver Federal Center, Denver, Colorado 80225

Region 9, Regional Administrator, Federal Highway Administration, 450 Golden Gate Avenue, Box 36096, San Francisco, California 94102 (415) 556-3895

Region 10, Regional Administrator, Federal Highway Administration, Room 412, Mohawk Building, 222 S.W. Morrison Street, Portland, Oregon 97204 (503) 221-2065

URBAN MASS TRANSPORTATION ADMINISTRATION

Region I, Office of the UMTA Representative, Urban Mass Transportation Administration, Transportation Systems Center, Technology Building, Room 277, 55 Broadway, Boston, Massachusetts 02142 (617) 494-2055

Region II, Office of the UMTA Representative, Urban Mass Transportation Administration, 26 Federal Plaza, Suite 1809, New York, New York 10007 (212) 264-8162

Region III, Office of the UMTA Representative, Urban Mass Transportation Administration, Mall Building, Suite 1214, 32t Chestnut Street, Philadelphia, Pennsylvania 19106 (215) 597-0407

Region IV, Office of UMTA Representative, Urban Mass Transportation Administration, 1720 Peachtree Road, Northwest, Suite 501, Atlanta, Georgia 30309 (404) 526-3948

Region V, Office of the UMTA Representative, Urban Mass Transportation Administration, 300 South Wacker Drive, Suite 700, Chicago, Illinois 60606 (312) 353-6005

Region VI, Office of the UMTA Repreventative, Urban Mass Transportation Administration, Federal Center, Suite 9E24, 1100 Commerce Street, Dallas, Texas 75202 (214) 749-7322

Region VII, Office of the UMTA Representative, Urban Mass Transportation Administration, c/o FAA Management Systems Division, Room 1564D, 601 East 12th Street, Kansas City, Missouri 64106 (816) 374-5567

Region VIII, Office of the UMTA Representative, Urban Mass Transportation Administration, Prudential Plaza, Suite 1822, 1050 17th Street, Denver, Colorado 80202 (303) 837-3242

Region IX, Office of the UMTA Representative, Urban Mass Transportation Administration, 450 Golden Gate Avenue, Box 36125, San Francisco, California 94102 (415) 556-2884

Region X, Office of the UMTA Representative, Urban Mass Transportation Administration, 1321 Second Avenue, Suite 5079, Seattle, Washington (206) 442-0590

...tion of impact statements. Under A-95, review of the proposed project in the case of federally assisted projects (Part I of A-95) generally takes place prior to the preparation of the impact statement. Therefore, comments on the environmental effects of the proposed project that are secured during this stage of the A-95 process represent inputs to the environmental impact statement.

2. In the case of direct Federal development (Part II of A-95), Federal agencies are required to consult with clearinghouses at the earliest practicable time in the planning of the project or activity. Where such consultation occurs prior to completion of the draft impact statement, comments relating to the environmental effects of the proposed action would also represent inputs to the environmental impact statement.

3. In either case, whatever comments are made on environmental effects of proposed Federal or federally assisted projects by clearinghouses, or by State and local environmental agencies through clearinghouses, in the course of the A-95 review should be attached to the draft impact statement when it is circulated for review. Copies of the statement should be sent to the agencies making such comments. Whether those agencies then

left to the discretion of the commenting agency depending on its resources, the signif cance of the project, and the extent to whic its earlier comments were considered in pre paring the draft statement.

4. The clearinghouses may also be use by mutual agreement, for securing review of the draft environmental impact state ment. However, the Federal agency may wis to deal directly with appropriate State local agencies in the review of impact state ments because the clearinghouses may b unwilling or unable to handle this phase the process. In some cases, the Governor ma have designated a specific agency, other tha the clearinghouse, for securing reviews of pact statements. In any case, the clearing houses should be sent copies of the impa statement.

5. To aid clearinghouses in coordinatir State and local comments, draft statemen should include copies of State and loc agency comments made earlier under th A-95 process and should indicate on the sum mary sheet those other agencies from whic comments have been requested, as specifie in Appendix I of the CEQ Guidelines.

APPENDIX C

Environmental Impact Statement Guidelines

or reviewing and commenting on environmental statements
by other Federal Agencies

Region X
Environmental Protection Agency
Seattle, Washington
April, 1973

(Abstract)

CONTENT OF ENVIRONMENTAL STATEMENTS*

SECTION II

* The following section "Content of Environmental Statements" is
a Regional interpretation of Section 102(2)(c) of the National
Environmental Policy Act. It must be realized that this
interpretation and these guidelines do not constitute EPA policy,
nor are they requirements under the National Environmental Policy
Act. They are based solely on the experience of EPA's Region X.

CONTENT OF ENVIRONMENTAL STATEMENTS
(Referring to Section 102 (2)(c) of PL-91-190)

Point (1) requires a description of primary and secondary impact on the environment including impacts on aesthetics, and aquatic and terrestrial ecosystems.

This requires a detailed description of the proposed action. It must include specifics of area involved, resources involved, what physical changes are proposed, what ecological systems will be altered and in what time frame these changes will occur. For example, a proposal for a reservoir project, power plant, or other facility, must include quantities of water stored, amounts and schedules of releases, changes in water quality including temperature, aquatic resources affected, tail water fluctuations, diversion points and amounts, quality of return flows if irrigation uses are involved, any exchange-of-flow arrangements, resource losses in reservoir area, and any other physical change which will have a significant impact. If a hydroelectric plant is to be constructed by a public utility company subject to license by the Federal government then information on such a facility should be included in the description.

This section also requires a description of the environmental interrelationship in the direct project area and the total affected area -- however extensive it may be. A major action, such as a storage reservoir, a pipeline, mining or logging operation, road construction, and recreation development or navigation works may not only affect air, soil, vegetation, and water quality in the immediate project area but may also be the inducement needed for industrial, recreational, or agricultural development with attendant environmental impacts.

Point (2) requires a description of any probable impact on the environment, including impact on ecological systems such as wildli♦ fish, and marine life.

The CEQ Guidelines state that significant actions include those which may have both beneficial and detrimental effects "even if, on the balance, the agency believes that the effect will be beneficial." Therefore, the agencies proposing action must consider and report all alterations to existing conditions whether or not they are deemed beneficial or detrimental. Since the Environmental Protection Agency is directly responsible for reviewing and commenting on air and water quality, solid wastes management, pesticides, noise, and radiation, the statements must include the anticipated changes in environmental quality in terms of the parameters commonly used to evaluate each of these areas.

Point (3) requires the responsible agency to study, develop and describe appropriate alternatives to recommended courses of action in any proposal which involves unresolved conflicts concerning alternative uses of available resources. Sufficient analysis of such alternatives and their costs and impact on the environment should accompany the proposed action through the agency review process in order not to foreclose prematurely options which might have less detrimental effects.

This requires not only complete alternatives which would accomplish the objective with less impact, but also non-structural alternatives and those that include elimination of certain "high environmental impact" aspects of the proposed action. Most actions involve a number of potential areas where an imaginative approach could lessen adverse environmental impacts while still meeting a majority of the projected needs. An environmental statement should describe these alternatives in such a manner that reviewers can independently judge if the environmental impact results from trying to gain maximum economic return or are inherent to the whole project.

Point (4) requires an assessment of the relationship between local short-term uses of man's environment and the maintenance and enhancement of long-term environmental productivity. The agency is required to assess their proposed action for cumulative and long-term effects on the environment.

The project or action must be evaluated in terms of use of renewable and non-renewable resources. In effect, the proposing agency must show who is paying the "environmental cost," the people who presently gain the benefits or future generations who may only be left with the cost. Most significant resource based actions have a long-term effect since there is a foreclosure of choices for future generations. For example, filling estuaries may provide additional land space for development but foreclose future choice of use and eventually impair the ability of the estuaries to support its normal biota.

Point (5) requires description of any irreversible and irretrievable commitment of resources.

For example, construction of a storage reservoir, filling or dredging of estuaries, construction of highways and pipelines are, for practical purposes, irretrievable commitments since such actions generally commit future generations to continue similar use. Also, appropriation of water through water rights, channel aligning, construction of major industrial operations, all are basically irreversible since the cost is such that removal is unlikely. Irreversible damage can also result from accidents such as oil spills. The risk of such occurrences should be discussed.

Point (6). The Council on Environmental Quality Guidelines include a Point 6 indicating, where appropriate, a discussion of problems and objections raised by local entities in the review process should be included.

The purpose of this is twofold. It encourages the proposing agency to contact and communicate with these groups and it provides reviewers a reference to groups who may have personal knowledge of the impact of the proposal.

GENERAL GUIDELINES

SECTION III

The following are general comments directed toward EPA's six areas of expertise based on legislation regarding programs administered by this agency. These are to be used in conjunction with the comments on specific types of Federal actions (Sect. IV) to stimulate environmental awareness and to aid in assessment of t[]broad range of impacts. These comments are not to be used as a checklist; they are only designed as guidelines. We have not incl[] a separate section specifically devoted to adverse impacts, but rather have used a broad category to cover all types and severity of environmental impacts. The reason for this approach is that we feel NEPA intended the impact statement to provide enough informat[] that adverse impacts will be clearly evident. This does not mean that adverse impacts should not be identified as such, but rather that all impacts should be presented in sufficient detail to allow the reviewer to independently determine the severity of these impacts.

A. Water Quality

1. The Federal Water Pollution Control Act of 1965, as amende[] authorized the individual states to adopt water quality standards [] protect the designated uses of water. After being adopted by the states, these standards were submitted to the Federal Water Polluti[] Control Administration of the Department of the Interior (now transferred to EPA) for approval. Standards generally were in the form of state regulations which set levels of water quality criteria such as dissolved oxygen, total coliform organisms, temperature, and other parameters. These criteria are legally enforceable requirements. The water quality standards of each State are promulgated by and available from that State environmental agency. The 1972 amendments to the Federal Water

lution Act preserve the existing standards and continue the
ndards program.* It required the states to re-examine their water
lity standards by April 18, 1973 and to revise them in ways
ntified by EPA.

Some of the key principles ennunciated by the Federal Courts (see
endix J) in the application of 102(2)(C) of the National
ironmental Policy Act in some of the listed cases to a significant
ree have been modified or superseded by the impact of the
visions contained in Section 511, The Federal Water Pollution
trol Act Amendments of 1972 (Public Law 92-500 enacted into
on October 18, 1972). Section 511(c)(2) of the Public Law
500 reads:

"Nothing in the National Environmental Policy Act of 1969
(83 Stat. 852) shall be deemed to--

"(A) authorize any Federal agency authorized to license or permit
the conduct of any activity which may result in the discharge of
a pollutant into the navigable waters to review any effluent
limitation or other requirement established pursuant to this
Act or the adequacy of any certification under Section 401 of
this Act; or

'(B) authorize any such agency to impose, as a condition precedent
to the issuance of any license or permit, any effluent
limitation other than any such limitation established pursuant
to this Act."

readers attention is called to the excellent compilation,
.egislative History of the Water Pollution Control Act Amendments
1972," together with Section-by-Section Index prepared by the
ronmental Policy Division of the Congressional Research Service
he Library of Congress, Volumes 1 and 2, Committee Print, 93d
ress, 1st Session, Serial No. 93-1, printed for the use of the
te Committee on Public Works, January 1973. The legislative
ory as contained in these documents contains the important
anatory materials relevant to all the provisions in P.L. 92-500,
uding Section 511. The Committee print can be purchased from
Superintendent of Documents, U.S. Government Printing Office,
ington, D.C. 20402, Volume 1 for $5.55, domestic postpaid, and
me 2 for $3.70, domestic postpaid.

---

2. For the reviewer to assess the effects of a project on the
r quality, the impact statement should include detailed information
he present biological, chemical, and hydrologic characteristics of

the water body, and should relate such knowledge to the establishe
water quality standards.

    a. Biological factors include flora and fauna that exist
or are dependent on the water body. The objective here is to rela
the water body to the local environment and to depict its importan
in the ecosystem of the project area.

    b. Chemical parameters of interest include the criteria
established in the state water quality standards as well as any otl
parameters which may be of significance in assessing the project's
impacts on water. This is important since it is often the changes
in micronutrients or other factors which affect biological growth
which significantly affect the water quality of the stream after
construction of the project.

    c. Hydrologic characteristics include such information as
high and low streamflows, occurrence of floods, flood plain
characteristics, groundwater flows, tributaries, natural drainage
channels, and alterations to natural hydrologic conditions which
will result from the project's construction and operation.

    3. The statement should provide detailed information on the
expected effects of the project on water quality, in terms of the
physical, chemical, and biological changes which will occur due to
the project.

    4. The statement should assess the impacts of the project on
water quality, in terms of applicable state water quality criteria
and should present sufficient information to allow the reviewer to
decide whether any of these impacts can be considered adverse.
Specific impacts to the identified uses of water, such as swimming
fish propagation, and water supply, should be stated.

5. If the project's construction or operation will result in conditions which would violate applicable water quality standards, these conditions should be spelled out in detail and should be analyzed in terms of the reason for their occurrence and possible methods to mitigate potential adverse effects of such violations.

6. Water quality should also be related in the statement to the existing ecosystems and the changes which will occur as a result of the project.

7. If the proposed action will affect drinking water supply, the impact statement should so state. U.S. Public Health Service Drinking Water Standards which apply to the water supply should be stated and compared to water quality resulting under post-project conditions.

B. Air Quality

1. What are the types and quantities of air pollutants that will be emitted as a result of the proposed action or alternatives to the proposed action. Inventories of pollutant emissions should be as detailed as possible including the point of pollutant discharge into the ambient air and stack parameters and concentrations if applicable.

2. Will the proposed action or alternatives to the proposed action result either directly (primary impact) or indirectly (secondary impact) in air pollutant concentrations exceeding national ambient air quality standards promulgated by the Administrator of the Environmental Protection Agency pursuant to Section 109 of the 1970 amendments to the Clean Air Act? Present standards are published in the April 30, 1971, issue of the Federal Register, pages 8186-8201. The procedures used for forecasting ambient pollutant concentrations should be described in detail.

3. Will the proposed action or alternatives to the proposed action result either directly or indirectly in air pollutant concentrations exceeding State or local ambient air quality standards which are more stringent than Federal standards or which are for pollutants for which Federal standards have not been established? As in 2., the procedures used for forecasting ambient pollutant concentrations should be fully described.

4. Is the proposed action consistent with air quality management measures included in State-adopted plans for achieving and maintaining national ambient air quality standards? Plans for the four States within Region X are available for review at the EPA Regional Office or at the office of the relevant State agencies:

   Alaska -- Department of Environmental Conservation

   Idaho -- Department of Environmental Protection and Health

   Oregon -- Department of Environmental Quality

   Washington -- Department of Ecology

5. Will the proposed action or alternatives to the proposed action result in the violation of State and/or local air pollution control emission regulations?

6. Is the proposed action in conformance with applicable Federal standards of performance for new stationary sources, as defined by Section 111 of the 1970 amendments to the Clean Air Act? Federal new source performance standards for steam generators, portland cement plants, sulfuric acid plants, nitric acid plants and municipal incinerators are published in the December 23, 1971, issue of the Federal Register, pages 24876-24895. EPA expects to promulgate during 1973 new source performance standards for other emission source categories.

7. Is the proposed action in conformance with applicable Federal emission standards for hazardous air pollutants, as defined in Section 112 of the 1970 amendments to the Clean Air Act? EPA expects to adopt standards for asbestos, beryllium, and mercury during 1973.

8. Does the alternative action selected for implementation minimize the extent of degradation of ambient air quality?

9. What consultation with State or local air pollution control agencies has occurred during planning of the proposed action and during preparation of the impact statement? If these agencies prepared written comments on the proposed action, these comments should be submitted as part of the impact statement.

C. Noise

The Noise Control Act of 1972 requires the EPA to prepare a criteria document regarding the effects of noise by August 1973 and to publish information on the levels of noise necessary to protect the public health by November 1973. The Act also requires EPA to set standards for several classes of equipment such as motor vehicles and construction equipment. Both the documents and the standards may lead to changes in these guidelines.

1. The following information is needed to evaluate the noise impact of the proposed action and the alternatives:

a. The existing and anticipated land uses near the project site or route that have a sensitivity to noise. (Particularly facilities in which speech or sleep occurs such as residences, motels, hotels, hospitals, schools, as well as recreational areas such as parks, campgrounds, nature preserves). What is the zoning and what does the comprehensive plan anticipate as the land use for undeveloped areas?

b. The existing noise levels adjacent to the project site or route. Sites should be selected both for their proximity to the projected noise source as well as for their noise sensitivity. L_{10}, L_{50} and L_{90} levels should be given in dbA units as well as the noise characteristics at the identified test sites. If the noise contains strong low frequency components, dbC scale measurements should also be made. Where necessary strong pure-tone components should be identified through full or one-third octave band measurements. The levels need not be presented as noise level contours. Methodology for determining these levels and qualifications of the investigator should be indicated.

c. The noise levels anticipated in these areas emanating from a completed project. L_{10}, L_{50} and L_{90} levels in dbA and/or dbC units should be documented for the same test sites at which existing levels were measured. (Peak noise levels should be determined because of their importance for sleep interference.) One statistical level should be presented as noise level contours. Methodology (noise prediction model) for determining these levels should be indicated, as well as experimental verification of the accuracy of the noise prediction model. Estimates of the maximum noise at nearest sensitive uses for each kind of construction equipment to be used should be stated. The numbers of each type of equipment should also be given.

      d. The criteria used to determine the impact of the predicted noise levels.

      (1) What increase is considered tolerable?

      (2) What levels are considered reasonable for various uses?

      (3) Upon what basis is this criteria established (i.e. sleep, speech, task interference or the right to a quiet environment)? The reference for the selected criteria should be cited.

      (4) State and municipal standards or ordinances which apply should be cited.

      e. What abatement means will be utilized to reduce noise from the completed project; what levels of attenuation will be achieved (abatement methods include barriers, berms, depression of the site, etc.)? The effectiveness of the abatement means should be demonstrated by the use of accepted noise prediction techniques.

      (1) What abatement means will be utilized to reduce noise during construction (i.e. acoustical modifications of construction equipment, regulation of hours and days of construction noise specifications for all equipment used on the project)?

      (2) What plans have been made to monitor the noise once the project is completed?

f.   What facilities will not be protected by the above abatement measures; what impact might this lack of protection have?

(1) Has consideration been given to procuring the additional land as a buffer zone or compensating for infringement of the use of the property?

(2) A cost benefit study of the trade off between noise reduction and land costs should be made where appropriate.

2. Recommended Criteria

a. Speech Communication

In residential areas or other areas where conversation out-of-doors is anticipated, it is desirable to be able to converse at distances up to 10 feet. As indicated in EPA-NTID 300.7 Effects of Noise on People, page 49, Figure 14, L_{50} levels should not exceed 55dBA. This would provide interior L_{50} levels of approximately 45dBA assuming open windows for ventilation.

b. Sleep Interference

For sleeping purposes maximum levels allowed are suggested peak levels since it is the peaks which cause arousal. EPA-NTID 300.7 Effects of Noise on People, page 68, Figure 17, indicates 50% of the people can be protected from awakening if interior peaks (L_{10}) do not exceed 50dBA. With windows open for ventilation, this suggests L_{10} outside of 60dBA to protect sleep.

Summary: Speech Communication L_{50} outside 55dBA

Sleep Interference L_{10} outside 60dBA
Note: Highway Research Board Report #117, page 30, Table 11, may also be used as a guide to recommended criteria.

c. Permissable Increase

Although a completed facility may not create levels in excess of those recommended, consideration must be given on a site by site basis to the increase from existing levels. EPA-NTID 300.: Community Noise, Chapter 5, indicates that the degree of annoyance experienced from intrusive sounds depends upon the noise level increase above pre-existing levels as well as upon the existing levels. Therefore some consideration must be given to the sites where levels will be increased substantially even if they do not exceed recommended maximum level specifications. As a general statement increases can be divided into three ranges, related to expected community response:

up to 5dBA increase - few complaints if gradual increas

5-10dBA increase - more complaints especially if conflict with sleeping hours

over 10dBA increase - substantial number of complaints

Generally no attention is needed if the increase is under 5dBA. Some consideration should be given to additional abatement measures or alternate routing or compensation if the range increase is 5-10dBA. If the increase is over 10dBA, the impact is considered serious and warrants close attention.

D. Solid Waste

Projects that will result in creation of solid waste, either during construction or as a result of operation of the completed facility, should address the following information.

1. The quantities and composition of solid waste which will be generated both in the construction process and as a result of operation of the facility.

2. Will any hazardous wastes be produced as a result of the proposed action?

3. Discuss the forecast for long term future waste loads resulting from the project. That is, what additional waste loads from population influx can be anticipated? Increased solid waste loads may overload existing facilities for handling residential, commercial and industrial wastes. Have local waste authorities been made fully aware of the new waste loads that will result from a rapid increase in population?

4. What plan has been developed for the storage, collection and disposal of all the different types of waste that will be generated?

    a. Where and how will wastes be stored?

    b. When will collections be made?

    c. What is disposal method?

    5. Has the potential for recycling or re-use of wastes generated by the project been fully investigated?

E. Radiation

The Atomic Energy Commission, as the licensing agency, has issued general guidance for the preparation of environmental reports for nuclear power plants. EPA reviewed this guidance and is in general agreement with the specific projections contained in the guide. A copy of the guide may be obtained from the AEC Directorate of Regulatory Standards, Washington, D.C. 20545.

F. Pesticides

The use of pesticides is a widespread practice included as a component of many projects or may be proposed as an independent project. To avoid repetition, we have included discussion of the general impacts of pesticides under the heading "Pesticides Projects" (Sect. IV, page 109). An outline of EPA's concerns can be found in this section. We ask the reader to review this section and to keep in mind that the concerns expressed relate to pesticides projects of any scale; the points raised apply equally well to routine use of pesticides for clearing of brush along highway routes to eradication of agricultural pests on an area-wide basis.

APPENDIX D

ENVIRONMENTAL IMPACT STATEMENT
Whitford Avenue Extension Subdivision
Whitestown, New York
1974

by
IMPACT CONSULTANTS
507 East Fayette Street
Syracuse, New York

for
THE BAILEY ASSOCIATION
124 Bleecker Street
Utica, New York

SUMMARY

Impact Consultants finds that there are no anticipated major adverse environmental impacts from the development of the 12-acre, 24-lot subdivision known as the Whitford Avenue Extension in the Town of Whitestown, New York. Primary findings include: several of the lot sites would be unsuited for homesites; wooded lots are incompatible with any fill operations and residual trees will rot withstand the impact of development without specific provision for their survival; hydrologic impact on the Sauquoit and Oriskany Creeks flood characteristics will be minimal, but on the immediate wetland site are considerable. Impact of the development on traffic, noise, recreation and the existing human environment, and impact of the environment on the proposed development are minor. Recommendations for amelioration or avoidance of adverse interactions are included.

There is no single adverse impact which would preclude development. On balance, consideration of the many minor adverse impacts raise doubts as to the advisability of continuation of site development for subdivision purposes, but must be weighed against several beneficial impacts: the immediate adverse and beneficial impacts are to be primarily incumbent upon adjacent residents.

1. The environmental impacts of the proposed action, completion of the Whitford Avenue Extension Subdivision in the Town of Whitestown, New York, which will significantly affect the quality of the environment are of several types, and cannot be categorically classified as being all beneficial or adverse. None are considered "major" impacts, that is, being disruptive of the local or regional watershed, vegetational, or zoological ecosystems, but severe impact would be, and already has been, established on-site.

   1.1 The environment is the southeastern portion of a wetland site, primarily forested swampland, which is situated on the divide between Oriskany and Sauquoit Creeks, immediately north of the southern Town boundary in Oneida County.

      1.11 Nearly the entire area was heavily forested before the present development began.

         1.11a The remaining forest areas have a relatively even-aged hardwood stand, predominantly in the large pole-size class, 8-12" dbh, and roughly 50 to 60 years of age, with scattered older, open-grown trees especially near the boundaries. The stand apparently results from the site having been cleared in the past, but the soil profile indicates that it was not cultivated. Sugar maple and beech predominate on the better-drained areas, grading to a predominance of red maple, elm, and hemlock on the poorer drained areas, with several other hardwood species scattered throughout.

         1.11b This wooded wetland forest type supports diverse ground flora and is an important habitat for many bird species. But, because it is widely represented in the general area, it is doubtful that any unique or rare species will be threatened by this development alone. Previously-cleared portions of this swampland support a cattail marsh community, but the very small portions of this on the site have already been filled.

         1.11c The extensive wetland just north and west of the site provides a major breeding ground for mosquitos, which will cause a substantial nuisance especially in any remaining wooded portions of the residential lots. This may prompt residents to remove the remaining forest cover to avoid resorting to heavy use of insecticides around their outdoor living areas.

1.12 The soils of the area are in the Lima-Kendaia-Lyons catena of predominantly silt loams on 0-3 percent slopes, derived from calcareous glacial till. Much of the area has a fine sandy loam surface soil, apparently resulting from local deposition, overlying more typical and less permeable silt to silty-clay loams.

    1.12a Such soils generally have fair to good stability, good bearing capacity and, on the gentle slopes here, moderately low erosion hazard.

    1.12b The principal limitation is seasonal to prolonged wetness. Roughly 30 percent of the area, on the slightly higher ridges is judged to be in the low range of the moderately well-drained Lima series with moderate limitations due to seasonal wetness; 30 percent, on the near flat areas, in the somewhat-poorly drained Kendaia series with greater limitations for development due to seasonal wetness; and 30 percent, in slightly depressed areas, especially in Lots 2, 3, 4, 19, 20 and 21, in the poorly-drained Lyons series with severe limitations due to prolonged wetness (Soil Conservation Service, 1972).

        Very poorly-drained soils, wet most of the year, come into the area at the southwest and northeast corners, especially lots 12 and 24, but have already largely been filled in (1.23) and are close to the area along most of its north boundary.

1.13 The geologic history of the area indicates that these soils are derived from glacial outwash, till, and lacustrine material deposited during the Wisconsin Glaciation, and are underlain by shales (Pearson, et al, 1960). The topography is gentle, with slight relief (535 to 545 feet above msl) and, locally, differences in elevation of one or two feet can be sufficient to allow substantial differences in vegetation development.

1.14 The climate of the area is characterized by cold winters and warm to hot summers, with precipitation distributed fairly evenly throughout the year (Black, 1974).

    1.14a Analysis of climatological data (Black, 1974) reveals that there is normally a substantial soil moisture deficit in the late summer as a result of high evapotranspiration demand and fairly constant precipitation: thus forested areas which retain water can be expected to be more capable of storing potential floodwaters from summer thunderstorms in the latter part of the summer than in the spring or late fall. Maximum annual floods on the Creeks are the result of snowmelt.

1.14b Data on wind are not immediately available from the
Utica airport. Data from Griffiss Air Force Base, which
also located in the Mohawk Valley, should therefore be
applicable to this site. The general prevailing winds over
the State are from the west, with a southwest component
present in the warmer months and a northwest component
in the winter months (Pack, 1960). The channeling effect
of the Mohawk Valley, however, prevents the southwesterly
flow from being felt at the surface, and the wind roses for
all seasons show strong flows along east-west and northeast
and northwest axes. Table 1 summarizes the wind situation.

TABLE 1 – Wind Patterns for Griffiss Air Force Base
in percent of time observed and average
wind speed (Beaufort Scale).

Season	Direction of Wind								
	N	NE	E	SE	S	SW	W	NW	Calm
Spring	6	3	13	18	4	4	28	16	8
	3	2	3	3	2	3	3	3	0
Summer	5	3	10	16	6	6	19	14	21
	3	2	2	2	3	3	3	3	0
Fall	6	3	12	32	6	5	21	12	3
	3	2	3	3	3	3	3	2	0
Winter	15	2	16	19	4	4	28	15	7
	3	2	3	3	3	3	4	4	0

Beaufort Scale: 0 = 1 mph; 1 = 1-3 mph; 2 = 4-7 mph;
3 = 8-12 mph; 4= 13-18 mph.

1.15 Hydrology of the Oriskany and Sauquoit Creeks watersheds differ
(Black, 1974).

1.15a Oriskany Creek experiences local flooding, particularly at
its confluence with the Mohawk River during the spring thaw,
and also some local, temporary high water as a result of
heavy, usually localized precipitation.

1.15b Sauquoit Creek, however, constitutes a major flood hazard
from both types of storms, the natural spring thaw type, and
the artificially-enhanced thunderstorm which provides
excess runoff to the mainstem owing to watershed configu-
ration, excessively-drained soils near the channel, and
encroachments on the flood plain.

The proposed subdivision, situated on the divide, has
about 8 acres in the Oriskany drainage, constituting
0.01 percent of that watershed; and about 4 acres in the
Sauquoit Creek watershed, representing less than 0.01
percent of its total. The approximately 8 acres of the
proposed subdivision that would occupy swamp land constitute about 5.4 percent of the total 147-acre wetland
according to the Utica West Quadrangle (Geological
Survey, 1955).

1.16   Other aspects of the environment include noise, air quality, and
         water quality.

         1.16a   The noise environment of the area is typical of exurban
                  areas (45 to 50 dBA) except when subjected to the noise
                  produced by aircraft using the nearby Oneida County
                  Airport. One jet flying to the west of the site produced
                  noise levels of 55 dBA on the site. These noise levels
                  would not usually be considered objectionable in resi-
                  dential areas (Housing and Urban Development, 1971).

         1.16b   No air quality data are available for the Whitestown area.
                  Data for Utica are not applicable since this station is
                  located in a commercial and industrial area (Department
                  of Environmental Conservation, 1973). The site is located
                  in a level 2 Ambient Air Quality Standard classification
                  area (Department of Environmental Conservation, no date),
                  but is immediately east of a level 3 area. In all probability
                  the air quality in the area is "good". A one-day on-site
                  investigation showed no noticeable air pollution or sources
                  of pollution other than residences and highways.

         1.16c   Analysis of water from the swamp, in the vicinity of the
                  north property line and the interceptor sewer right of way,
                  reveals typical forest wetland conditions, with near neutral
                  pH, high (31 ppm) and low (1.5 ppm) dissolved oxygen
                  contents. The expected low pH is precluded by the high
                  alkalinity value (254 ppm). Analysis of the stream drain-
                  ing the entire swamp, where it crosses Clark Mills Road,
                  revealed restoration to near-normal dissolved oxygen
                  (6.4 ppm) and carbon dioxide (12 ppm) levels. Hardness
                  of both samples was low (ca. 17 ppm), due entirely to
                  calcium, moderately high iron (ca. 1 ppm) and silica
                  (3.5 to 5 ppm) contents indicate prolonged contact of
                  these surface waters with exposed soil material.

1.17   There are no known historical, mineral, or unique ecological resources
         on or beneath the site.

1.2 The action, completion of the proposed Whitford Avenue Extension Subdivision, is the landscaping and construction necessary to erect 24 one- or two-story, single-family residences on one half-acre lots, as described by Parry and Colangelo, Licensed Land Surveyors, dated 1971, and revised March 10, 1973 (Figure 1).

    1.21   Twenty of the lots are to be rectangular, approximately 160 feet deep and 90 feet fronting the Avenue, and 4 are to be irregularly-shaped surrounding the turn-around at the end of the Avenue.

    1.22   Between lots 19 and 20 on the north side, there is to be a 60-foot reservation for a street linking Whitford Avenue with the next street north to preclude a cul-de-sac. This link would be located approximately along the divide between the two major drainages (1.15c).

    1.23   Fill has already been accomplished

        1.23a   on lot 24 where the local drainage has been blocked and a 12-inch culvert has been installed from the back line to Whitford Avenue, linking with the existing storm sewers along Whitford Avenue, and

        1.23b   on lot 12, where a portion of the wetland has been obliterated by fill and ditched to provide drainage from the site.

    1.24   Sanitary sewers, primary road construction, and tree-felling at house locations on the south-side lots has been completed as of the date of investigation (June 12, 1974). Approval for continuation of the subdivision awaits affirmative action from the Department of Environmental Conservation (Luz, 1974), and the Oneida County Planning Department (Kennedy, 1974), in view of the concern over potential contribution to flooding on Sauquoit Creek by unregulated and haphazard development on the watershed (1.35).

        1.24a   The County interceptor sewer already disrupts the natural drainage of the wetland to the northwest, and

        1.24b   the abandoned sewage treatment plant has been a likely contributor to accelerated eutrophication of the wetland.

    1.25   Impact Consultants assumes that the developer has provided for adequate water supplies, and has complied with appropriate state and local building and health codes, and has not undertaken investigation of capacity of community services to assimilate additional loads.

128

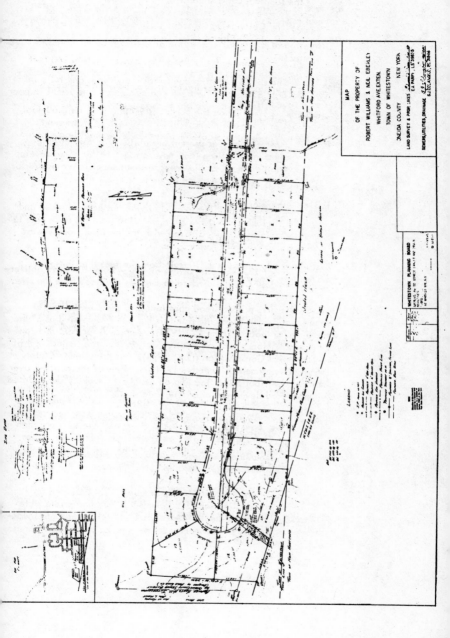

1.3   The impacts on the environment by the proposed action are varied and
        include potential disruption of the vegetative ecosystem, temporary dis-
        turbance to soils on site, disturbance to the wetland, and modification
        of the several aspects of the environment which relate to human comfort.

        1.31   Disruption of the forest vegetation on-site can be expected to have
                two effects:

                1.31a   The shallow rooting due to soil conditions and tall, thin
                        form of most of the trees can be expected to result in poor
                        stability and survival if the stand is heavily thinned for
                        residential development; and

                1.31b   most of the trees present are unlikely to tolerate the
                        substantial filling that may be required for home develop-
                        ment on much of the area, without specific provisions for
                        their protection, such as wells or drain tiles:

                1.31c   therefore, most of the forest cover will probably have to
                        be removed for the home development as planned and can
                        probably be left safely only on the back portions of the
                        lots where little disturbance may be necessary.

        1.32   Disturbance to the soils will result from the fact that these are
                moderately erodable and wet:

                1.32a   were steep slopes present, considerable erosion and
                        sedimentation would be evident following vegetative
                        clearing but, in absence of such, only minimal soil
                        movement is anticipated and may be easily controlled
                        by seeding soon after initial disturbance (Bradley, 1974);

                1.32b   it is estimated that substantial site modification – drainage
                        and/or fill – will be needed for residential development
                        on about 70 percent of the site, especially if basements
                        are only partially below grade and landscaping requires
                        that backfill be employed. However, the soils are high
                        in lime, quite fertile, and relatively free of stones, so
                        should support good lawns and other residential vegeta-
                        tion wherever adequately drained.

        1.33   The hydrologic disturbance is naturally "graded" between consider-
                ations of the immediate wetland site, the swamp to the north and
                west, and the larger watersheds of which the land is a part (1.15).

130

able, in the form of

i) restriction of drainage from the swamp through lot 24 and the 12-inch culvert described above (1.23a);

ii) more rapid surface runoff from the expected 40 percent of the area that will be rendered impervious by roads, drives, roofs, etc.;

iii) input of nutrients to the swamp as a result of leaching of fertilizer from lawns and gardens, pet droppings, etc.; and

iv) decreased evapotranspiration loss from the development site as a result of decreased vegetated and open-water surfaces.

The impacts of these changes are, it is noted, added onto the impact of the interceptor sewer (1.24a) and the sewage treatment plant (1.24b). In other terms, the addition of more nutrients would accelerate eutrophication still further, and the total hydrologic impacts would compensate each other in some instances, and reinforce one another in others.

1.33b Impact on the Oriskany Creek watershed system is likely to be minimal, particularly in view of the fact that drainage from the bulk of the development (1.15c) trends northwest through the sewage treatment plant which already has imposed both hydrologic and water quality impacts and will continue to do so in spite of abandonment.

1.33c Impact on the Sauquoit Creek watershed system is also minimal, although it is recognized that extensive development of this type could have an additive adverse impact in the long run, particularly in view of the existing flood problem (1.15). The increased surface runoff from paved surfaces would be undetectable in the main stream, and may in fact be compensated for by the restriction of flow at lot 24 (1.33a i).

1.33d Excess storm runoff may cause local flooding on-site, just as intense storms presently cause the water level in the swamp to rise since there is no subsurface storage. In fact, when full, the site presently behaves hydrologically as if it were already paved, that is, there is no large storage potential other than on the surface. This applies to winter conditions, as well, for swamps have been found to be frozen to a greater depth than an open field, hardwood and spruce stands (Colman, 1953).

1.34   The impact of the development of 24 home sites on the air quality
        of the area and noise will be small.

        1.34a   The primary impacts will be from home heating, which
                 would probably be oil, and from increased automobile
                 traffic. In our opinion, these sources in themselves
                 would not significantly affect in a measurable way, the
                 ambient air quality of the area. Note, however, that a
                 large number of small developments such as proposed here
                 would have a significant, additive impact on air quality
                 of the area.

        1.34b   The additional noise introduced into the area would have
                 no noticeable effect on the general noise level of the
                 surrounding residenfial area since the background noise
                 level would be at the same level as that generated by the
                 use of the proposed sites.

1.35   Modifications to several additional environmental factors will con-
        stitute impacts which should be recognized. Impact Consultants did
        not pursue detailed investigation of these impacts, but recognize that
        they may include:

        1.35a   impact of construction activity on the existing residents of
                 Whitford Avenue (2.31);

        1.35b   impact of additional need for services in the Town of
                 Whitestown, such as for schools, police and fire protection,
                 snow removal, street repair, and garbage collection, as
                 well as other services (1.25);

        1.35c   impact on the potential use of the power line right of way
                 and the old railroad grade as recreational and open-space
                 facilities (1.36); and

        1.35d   impact on the existing subdivision in terms of traffic, noise,
                 and air pollutants from the increased traffic along Whitford
                 Avenue (2.32).

        With the exception of the first-mentioned, which is temporary, Impact
        Consultants believes that it would be helpful to examine the plan for
        the subdivision in light of 1) existing plans for wetlands management,
        2) any overall land use plan for the Town of Whitestown, 3) the general
        land use plan, when available, for the Sauquoit Creek watershed, and
        4) specific recreation, open space, and transportation plans for the
        region in order to fully assess the environmental impact of this (or any
        other) subdivision: such an examination of the impact of policy and
        programs is beyond the scope of this environmental impact statement.

1.36   If the proposed Westmoreland Arterial shown on the Town's Zoning Districts map (undated) is to be constructed on the existing railroad and/or power line rights of way immediately adjacent to the proposed subdivision's southern boundary or through its center (Kennedy, 1974), two future impacts should be weighed:

     1.36a   engineering consideration of drainage of the proposed arterial could either aid in drying the site or in completely inundating it, and

     1.36b   noise and degraded air quality would be greater impacts of the arterial on the subdivision owing to its close proximity (Housing and Urban Development, 1971).

     The summary impact would be intolerable to many residents of the subdivision if completed.

1.37   Impact of the surrounding, somewhat hostile environment on the proposed subdivision should be considered:

     1.37a   the air quality of the area is subjectively "good" (1.16b) and is not detrimental to the use of the site for housing;

     1.37b   the noise environment is not adverse for residential use (1.16a), but

     1.37c   the insect, moisture, and odor characteristics of the swamp will have an adverse impact on future residents which may be of sufficiently high level to render the area less than ideally suitable for residential use.

The major adverse impacts are summarized and discussed in detail below.

2.   The major adverse impacts of the proposed development on the environment are those associated with the local ecosystem, local hydrology, and the residents of the existing adjacent subdivision.

2.1   The disruption of the existing forest cover as described above (1.31) poses a dilemma, for the homes cannot be developed with all the trees retained on-site owing to their inevitable demise as a result of inability to withstand sudden exposure (1.31a) and/or filling over the existing land surface (1.31b). Nor can the existing forest-grown trees be retained with any expectation that they would suffice as desirable shade trees. It is highly probable, then, that if the subdivision is built, there will be a severe adverse impact on (elimination of) the existing forest vegetation: with a few exceptions, the stand does not contain merchantable timber, and its value from that standpoint is low. The open-grown trees might be retained for shade trees. As a site for recreation, the existing stand is of value primarily to those who live adjacent to it, but its mosquito-breeding and odor-producing potential would be diminished (for near-by residents) by construction of the subdivision and this beneficial impact must be weighed against the adverse one just described.

2.2 Owing to slight redistribution of the drainage within the swamp, increased imperviousness of the site, and resultant adjustments to the water levels in the swamp, it is to be expected that vegetation along with altered water quality parameters will change. The adverse impact here will likely be that a small additional area adjacent to the swamp will become wetter as the developed site becomes drier, and somewhat deeper and more prolonged wetness will occur within the swamp's current limits. In fact, as noted, most of the adverse hydrologic impact has already taken place (1.23).

2.3 Adverse impacts on residents of the existing subdivision are minimal (1.34; 1.35) except for traffic:

2.31 during construction Whitford Avenue residents would suffer the annoyances of dust, noise, and truck traffic. The latter two would be during daylight hours only, and the former could be ameliorated by sprinkling.

2.32 Traffic volume along Whitford Avenue will eventually nearly double (Kennedy, 1974) with concomitant increases in congestion and noise exposure (not level).

3. Alternatives to the proposed action are likely to produce more environmental impact.

3.1 The null alternative would, without question, have the minimal impact:

3.11 precluding further development of the site will result in eventual regrowth of vegetation on disturbed areas, and

3.12 hydrologic redistribution as described will be maintained since those changes have already taken place (1.23).

This alternative, however, is unrealistic without specific action to remove existing alterations to the landscape, particularly on lots 12 and 24, and such would have a temporary impact of considerable magnitude, and perhaps of some less severe lasting ones.

3.2 Several alternatives could be included with the general concept of maintaining the site in as "natural" a condition as possible:

3.21   as a recreation area;

3.22   as open space, or

3.23   as an entire wetland community preserved for study and wildlife and wildfowl preservation.

Impact Consultants believes that this is not a viable alternative in that, again, disturbance has already occurred to the site and the ecosystem has been (and will be) disrupted by the abandoned sewage treatment pond and the rights of way for the railroad, power line, and interceptor sewer.

3.3   Alternatives within the development include:

3.31   development of just the southside lots, however, the construction of the Westmoreland Arterial would bound this area closely (1.36); and

3.32   locating the connecting link road along the interceptor sewer right of way at the west end of the subdivision, or extending the road all the way through to Woods Highway.

3.4   Several additional alternatives are identifiable under the general heading of more intensive development, such as for public services, office parks, or light industrial sites. None are considered as viable alternatives and are not discussed further.

The relationships "between the short-term uses of man's environment and the maintenance and enhancement of long-term productivity" (National Environmental Policy Act, 1969, 42 USC 4321) must be considered in this case only from the standpoint of the potential use of the site as a resource. Its long-term productivity lies primarily in its ability to serve the needs of the community, either as open space and, perhaps, part of the wetland (which may be viewed as a resource complex involving vegetation, animals, and wildfowl) or developed land, as proposed, for continued production of tax revenues to the extent that such exceed costs of such use to the community. There are no known short-term or long-term potential uses which might yield greater benefit to the community in the form of resource exploitation, agricultural, or forest crops.

The only irreversible or irretrievable commitments of resources to be incurred if the subdivision is completed have been discussed above, and consist of major modification and perhaps elimination of the existing forest cover on the site.

LITERATURE CITED

Black, P. E. 1974. Environmental Hydrology and Management. Oneida County Department of Planning, Utica, New York. 68 pp.

Bradley, R. C. 1974. Development Plan Review of Whitford Avenue Extension. U.S. Department of Agriculture, Soil Conservation Service. 2 pp.

Colman, E. A. 1953. Vegetation and Watershed Management. The Ronald Press, New York. 412 pp.

Department of Environmental Conservation, 1973. New York State Air Quality Report: Continuous Monitoring System. BAQS-50, Albany, New York. 85 pp.

-------, no date. Map of "New York State Air Classifications": see also official compilation of codes, rules and regulations, Title 6, Chapter III, Subchapter A, Parts 256 and 257, Conservation Law.

Geological Survey, 1955. Utica West Quadrangle. $7\frac{1}{2}$-minute Topographic map. Washington, D.C.

Housing and Urban Development, 1971. Noise Assessment Guidelines. Washington, D.C HUD Report TE/NA 171. 35 pp.

Kennedy, J. G. 1974. Letter to P. Lambert, Oneida County Health Department, May 8.

Luz, J. F. 1974. Letter to P. Lambert, Oneida County Health Department, April 19.

Pack, B. A. 1960. Climate of New York. Number 60-30, Climate of United States. U.S. Government Printing Office. Washington, D.C. 29 pp.

Pearson, C. S., R. Feuer, and M. G. Cline, 1960. Oneida County Soils. Soil Association Leaflet 10, Cornell University, Ithaca, New York.

Soil Conservation Service, 1972. Soil Survey Interpretations of Soils in New York State. Department of Agronomy, Cornell University, Ithaca, New York, and U.S. Department of Agriculture, Syracuse, New York 543 pp.

A SELECTED, ANNOTATED BIBLIOGRAPHY
OF IMPORTANT ENVIRONMENTAL BOOKS

Compiled by Lee P. Herrington and Peter E. Black, 1973

ANDERSON, F. R. 1973. NEPA in the courts.
Johns Hopkins Press, Baltimore, Md. 324 pp.

Excellent account of Congressional handling of NEPA, and court decisions to date.

BABCOCK, R. F. 1966. The zoning game.
University of Wisconsin Press, Madison, Wisc. 202 pp.

An exceptionally well-written history of and attack on zoning.

BATES, M. 1961. The Forest and the Sea.
Mentor Books, N. Y. 216 pp.

A classic. A readable approach to an environmental continuum.

BATTAN, L. J. 1966. The Unclean Sky.
Doubleday-Anchor Books, Garden City, N.Y. 141 pp.

A general but sound discussion of air pollution: sources, movement, measurement.

BERNARDE, M. A. 1973. Our precious habitat.
W. W. Norton, & Co., Inc., New York. 448 pp.

A thought-provoking work on "an integrated approach to understanding man's effect on his environment."

BURNS, W. 1968. Noise and Man.
J. B. Lippincott Co., Philadelphia, Pa. 336 pp.

A detailed discussion of Noise physics and the physiological effects of noise.

BURTON, I., & R. W. KATES, Editors. 1965.
Readings in Resource Management and Conservation.
The University of Chicago Press, Chicago. 609 pp.

Selections from the environmental management classics.

CARR, D. E. 1966. Death of the Sweet Waters.
W. W. Norton & Co., N. Y. 257 pp.

A scare-type book on mistreatment of the water resource.

CARSON, R. 1962. Silent Spring.
(1964 printing) Crest Book t681, New York. 304 pp.

The book that launched the environmental era.

CLAWSON, M. 1963. Land and Water for Recreation.
   Rand McNally & Co., for Resources for the Future

   Particularly important for presentation of man-environment relationship

CLEARY, E. J. 1967. The ORSANCO Story.
   The Johns Hopkins Press, Baltimore, Md. 335 pp.

   *The complete history and technical detail of problems and solutions
   of the Ohio River Valley Water Sanitary Commission.*

COMMITTEE ON RESOURCES AND MAN, 1969. Resources and Man.
   W. H. Freeman and Co., Inc., San Francisco, Calif. 259 pp.

   *A valuable series of papers by experts on various resource topics
   as related to their use by man.*

COUNCIL ON ENVIRONMENTAL QUALITY, 1970 Environmental Quality.
   First Annual Report. USGPO, Washington, D. C. 326 pp.

   The first report was basically a problem analysis.

COUNCIL ON ENVIRONMENTAL QUALITY, 1971. The Second Annual Report on
   Environmental Quality.
   USGPO, Washington, D. C. 360 pp.

   Particularly instructive in matters legal.

COUNCIL ON ENVIRONMENTAL QUALITY, 1972. The Third Annual Report on
   Environmental Quality.
   USGPO, Washington, D. C. 450 pp.

   Largely a progress report, with lots to report.

COUNCIL ON ENVIRONMENTAL QUALITY. 1973. The Fourth Annual Report
   on Environmental Quality.
   USGPO, Washington, D. C. 499 pp.

   This zeroes in on particular problems.

DASMANN, R. F., 1962. Environmental Conservation.
   . John Wiley & Sons, Inc.

   The widely-used introductory text.

DASMANN, R. F., 1965. The Destruction of California.
   The MacMillan Co., Inc.,

   *Application of the above text's overview to the specific problems -
   of which there is a wide variety - in California.*

DEPARTMENT OF HEALTH, EDUCATION & WELFARE, 1969. Report of the Secretary's
   Commission on Pesticides and their relationship to environmental
   health. Washington D. C. 677 pp.

   Data - all you want - on the subject in the Subcommittee reports.

DETWYLER, T. R., ed. 1971. Man's Impact on the Environment.
McGraw-Hill Book Co., Inc., New York   731 pp.

*A collection of recent papers on the several categories of
man's impacts.*

DITTON, R. B., & T. I. GOODALE, eds. 1972. Environmental Impact
Analysis: Philosophy and Methods.
University of Wisconsin, Madison, Wisconsin 171 pp.

*Symposium papers, very brief, though some interesting &
valuable ideas are presented.*

DORFMAN, R., & N. S. DORFMAN., eds. 1972. Economics of the Environment.
W. W. Norton & Co., Inc., N. Y. 426 pp.

A collection of recent, selected papers.

EHRLICH, P. R. 1968. The Population Bomb.
Ballentine Books, Inc., N. Y. 223 pp.

*This important work, not without its errors of interpretation,
is diversified in its view of all natural resources and
population pressures.*

ELY, R. T. & G. S. WEHRWEIN 1964. Land Economics.
University of Wisconsin Press, Madison, Wisconsin

The classic in its field.

ENK, G. A. 1973. Beyond NEPA -- Criteria for Environmental Impact
Review. The Institute on Man and Science, Rensselaerville, N. Y.
140 pp.

A valuable current summary of State & Federal compliance with NEPA

FEDERAL REGISTER DIVISION, GSA. 1971, (revised annually). United States
Government Organization Manual, 1971 - 1972. National Archives and
Records Service U. S. Government Printing Office, Washington D. C.

A most valuable reference book.

GARVEY, G. 1972. Energy Ecology, Economy.
W. W. Norton & Co., Inc., N. Y. 235 pp.

*A thought-provoking work that calls for a "practical response to
an urgent environmental problem."*

GATES, P. W. 1968. History of Public Land Law Development.
U. S. Government Printing Office, Washington, D. C. 828 pp.

Basic data & history for the Public Land Law Review Commission.

GRAHAM, F. 1970. Since Silent Spring.
　　Houghton Mifflin Co., Boston, Mass 333 pp.

　　Documentation of the impact of Carson's book.

GRANGE, W. B. 1953. Those of the Forest.
　　Faber and Faber, London. 295 pp.

　　*A classic: perhaps the most beautiful & beautifully written book on
　　ecology.*

GROBSTEIN, C. 1965. The strategy of Life.
　　W. H. Freeman & Co., San Francisco, California 118 pp.

　　*A concise description of the whole spectrum of our environment
　　from macrocosm to microcosm.*

HELFRICH, H.W., ed. 1970. The Environmental Crisis
　　Yale University Press, New Haven, Conn. 187 pp.

　　*First of two collected papers from a Yale University Lecture
　　Series.*

HELFRICH, H.W., ed. 1970. Agenda for Survival (The Environmental Crisis - 2
　　Yale University Press, New Haven, Conn., 234 pp.

　　*Second. Both volumes consist of papers by leading contemporary
　　authorities.*

HERFINDAHL, O. C., and A. V. KNEESE, 1965. Quality of the Environment.
　　An Economic Approach to Some Problems in using Land, Water, and Air.
　　Johns Hopkins Press, Baltimore, Md. 96 pp.

　　*This Resources For the Future publication is a balanced, thoughtful
　　presentation of the breadth of environmental - economic problems,
　　but somewhat lacking in depth.*

HODGES. L. 1973. Environmental Polution.
　　Holt, Rinehart and Winston, Inc., N. Y. 370 pp.

　　Brief overviews of many pollution problems.

HOLWAY, J. G., & J. G. NEW, eds. 1972. Search for the Quality of Life:
　　The Challenge of the '70s.
　　State University College at Oneonta, N. Y. 205 pp.

　　Symposium papers.

HORNADAY, W. T. 1913. Our Vanishing Wildlife.
　　New York Zoological Society, New York.

　　A classic.

HOWE, C. W. 1971. Benefit-Cost Analysis for Water System Planning.
    AFU Water Resources Monograph 2, American Geophysical Union
    Washington, D. C. 144 pp.

    The most readable presentation of a rather complex topic.

INTERNATIONAL INSTITUTE FOR ENVIRONMENTAL AFFAIRS. 1972. Who
    Speaks for Earth?
    W. W. Norton & Co., Inc., New York. 173 pp.

    *The views of seven contemporary authorities on environmental
    problems.*

KAUFMAN, H. 1960. The Forest Ranger, a study in administrative
    behavior.
    The John Hopkins Press, Baltimore, Md. 259 pp.

    Inside the U. S. Forest Service.

LEOPOLD, A. 1949. A Sand County Almanac.
    Oxford University Press, New York   226 pp.

    A classic.

MARSH, G. P. 1885. The Earth as Modified by Human Action.
    Scribner & Sons., Inc., New York

    *A classic, but tough to read with small print & verbose
    footnotes.*

MEYERS, C. J., & A. D. TARLOCK 1971. Selected Legal and Economic
    Aspects of Environmental Protection.
    The Foundation Press, Inc., Mineola New York   410 pp.

    A valuable reference book.

MURDOCH, W. W., ed. 1971. Environment, Resources, Pollution, and
    Society.
    Sinauer Associates, Inc., Stamford, Conn.   440 pp.

    *A collection of papers in several categories of man-environment
    relations.*

NATIONAL SCIENCE BOARD, 1971. Environmental Science, Challenge
    for the Seventies.
    U. S. Government Printing Office, Washington D. C.   50 pp.

    Important historical reference.

ODUM, H. T. 1971. Environment, Power, and Society.
    John Wiley & Sons, Inc., New York   331 pp.

    The best in its field.

OSBORN, F. 1949. Our Plundered Planet.
    Little, Brown and Co., Boston, Mass. 217 pp.

    An early pessimistic classic.

.PIEL, G., 1961. Science in the Cause of Man.
    Alfred A. Knopf, New York

    *A frightening yet heartening account by the editor of
    Scientific American on governmental suppression of the
    scientific press.*

REITZE, A. W. 1972. Environmental Law I.
    North American International, Washington, D. C. 542 pp.

    A valuable reference.

STRAHLER, A. N., & A. H. STRAHLER, 1973. Environmental Geoscience:
    Interaction Between Natural Systems and Man.
    Hamilton Publishing Co., Santa Barbara, California   575 pp.

    One of the best-available introductory texts on the topic.

THOMAS, W. K., ed. 1956. Man's Role in Changing the Face of the
    Earth.
    University of Chicago Press, Chicago.   1193 pp.

    Symposium papers - a classic.

THORNE, W., ed. 1963. Land and Water Use. A symposium presented at
    the Denver meeting of the AAAS, December, 1961.
    American Association for the Advancement of Science,
    Washington D. C.

    Thoughts of leaders in the field.

TRUMAN, D. B., 1959. The Governmental Process.
    Alfred Knopf, Inc., New York

    An excellent presentation on the politics of interest groups.

UDALL, S. L. 1963. The Quiet Crisis.
    Avon. 224 pp.

    A classic

VOGT, W. 1948. Road to Survival.
    William Sloane Associates, New York

    *An early view of how to meet the problems of man-environment
    interactions.*